"I don't have the money"

Handling Your Financial Emergencies

Dan Keppel, MBA
The Working Millionaire: $2,000,000 Tax-FREE Wealth Reserve
Self-insure Self-fund

IAN Books

An IAN Books paperback

Published by
IAN Books
41 Watchung Plaza, B242
Montclair, NJ 07042

Copyright © Dan Keppel 2016

All rights reserved. No part of this book or its Interactive Internet CD can be reproduced, transmitted in any form or by any means, electronic or mechanical, including photocopying, recording, or by any information storage and retrieval system, without the written permission of the publisher.

Special sales for educational use by nonprofits.
IANBooksEditor@Yahoo.com

Cover: Română: Miinile unui iobag modern by TARE GHEORGHE

ISBN-13: 978-1537636702
ISBN-10: 1537636707
Library of Congress Control Number: 2016915503

Dewey 332.024

1. Finance, Personal 2. General
I. Keppel, Dan1948-. II. Title.

IAN Books at Amazon.com

Wealth Without Wall Street:
Buy Direct -- Avoid the Commissions, Fees, Loads

The Insiders' Guides to Buying Discount Financial Services:
Buy Direct and Save $3,000 Every Year

Drop Your Insurance:
Buy Only What You Need

Create Financial Freedom Using Your Wealth Reserve ™:
Fix your financial life

The Simple Financial Life:
How to get what you want without going into debt and living paycheck to paycheck

Build Wealth Without Extra Money or Time:
You don't need to budget or get an extra job

Leah's Money Book:
"I want to control my own money."

The Working Millionaire:
$2,000,000 Tax-FREE Wealth Reserve ™ Self-insure Self-fund

Build Your Own $2,000,000 Tax-FREE Wealth Reserve ™:
Self-insure Self-fund your lifestyle
Stop wasting $3,000 every year:
101
financial products **NOT** to buy and why

Your Investment Edge:
A Tax-FREE Growth and Income Account

Sign up for our Email Alerts at
www.TheInsidersGuides.com

FREE Wealth Building strategies

FREE money savings ideas

Learn about new direct-to-customer
products and services
from manufacturers that save you money

Contents

Let Uncle Sam help pay for emergencies   7

1. Create a tax-FREE investment account   11

2. A Simple, Easy and Wise Plan   27

3. 'Snoring' is the best way to create wealth!   41

4. Self-insure with your **Wealth Reserve**™   47
    There is no better protection than having assets

5. Create a self-funded 'Bank'   61
    Pay up to 40% less for any item

6. The Insider's Guide to Disability Insurance: 71
    Cash is a better plan

7. The Insider's Guide to Vehicle Insurance: 83
    Beware of double coverage

8. The Insider's Guide to Life Insurance: 97
    Do you need it?

9. The Insider's Guide to Homeowner's Insurance: 111
    Beware false coverage

10. The Insider's Guide to Health Insurance: 129
    Affordable health insurance

11. The Insider's Guide to Mutual Funds & Securities: 147
     Beware fees

12. The Insider's Guide for Women: 173
     Secure Your Financial Independence

13. The Insider's Guide to a Spending Plan: 183
     Who else will build wealth for you?

You are prepared for emergencies   196

Resources   202

Your Unbiased Advisor Network   204

The Author   209

FREE Wealth Building strategies
FREE savings ideas

Start your free
Email Alerts at
TheInsidersGuides.com/

Let Uncle Sam help pay for your emergencies

Cash is your best protection for emergencies
Use a tax-FREE account—**Save 30%** on income taxes.
Avoid securities **fees & charges taking up to 63%** of your money.
Accumulate $55,000, $250,000, even $1,000,000.

Don't let a financial emergency kill your financial dreams. Many financial plans have been destroyed by an unexpected, huge, catastrophic event that catches you without money. If your spouse is in an accident or your home burned or you die, how will your family move on from the devastation?

Most emergencies can be handled by a combination of cash and insurance. Because some events can have catastrophic impact on your life, you need insurance. However, having the *wrong kind of insurance* can destroy your life too. And certain situations demand cash since there is no or very expensive insurance available.

Insurance shifts the financial burden from you in exchange for regular premiums. Wealthy people have a large policy but it doesn't cost them big bucks. They carry the right kind of coverage —a form of "self-insurance"—so they pay low premiums for years. They use this premium savings to build their emergency fund in a tax-FREE account and Uncle Sam helps out on taxes.

They balance risk and reward so they save on the cost of insurance *over time*. They save premium for years in a tax-FREE account. Total catastrophic loss is a small risk. They are covered if their house burns down but use the savings to build cash. Since investing the money for your own gains instead of giving it to the insurance company will most likely produce a lower long term cost, partial self-insurance is their choice. Tax-FREE saves 30%.

I will show you how to do this for all your financial needs. For example, this strategy works for life insurance:

SBLI charged $384 for the same $300,000 30-year term policy that MetLife charged $983 for in 2009. Their financial strength ratings are A+ and their underwriting requirements are the same. The difference, $600, over 30 years is $17,970. If invested, that $600 can add $175,000 to YOUR assets when you need them. MetLife has to pay agents, Snoopy, high rents and expensive CEOs.

This is why most thrifty shoppers pick term over cash value life insurance. Cash value life insurance is NOT a good investment. It may be useful to wealthy people who have a huge estate tax bill but it is not a smart choice for replacing family income due to a premature death.

So in both examples, you are far better off buying insurance that allows you to create what I call a ***Wealth Reserve*™** than a low deductible liability or a cash value policy. Using the time value of money—compounding—you end up with more cash and the appropriate coverage.

And what about long-term health care insurance. Everyone is telling you to buy it but is it right for you? Is insuring a child's life a better move than helping them get started with money? When you invest for the future, do you use your IRS-approved tax shelter? Do you pay 2% or 0.20% of your investment dollars to build wealth? Do you use your tax shelters for college and medical expense savings?

I help you find the right answer for you. It doesn't make sense to give up 63% of your nest egg to your advisor who can't beat the market over time. Every unbiased study shows you can do better when investing for the long term. Only 2.5% of the Street's "professionals," who hand-pick a bunch of stocks (a mutual fund), are successful over time.

You could add another 30% to your ***Wealth Reserve*™** to cover your medical expenses not covered by Medicare. You do not need an advisor to take advantage of these shelters. In fact, you will end up with more by using a not-for-profit mutual fund firm and fee-only professionals.

By the end of this book you will have a complete answer to the question, "Are you prepared for financial emergencies." You will learn Warren Buffett's strategy to earn market returns of 10-12% in your legal tax shelters. You will learn how to avoid high fees and taxes on your investment earnings. You will have more cash.

We can earn 10-12% a year: We save up to 63% on fund costs http://www.moneychimp.com/features/market_cagr.htm and 30% on taxes. The wealthy avoid taxes. Many pay under **17% total** tax. Most of us pay 32.9%. Most corporations pay under 20%.

The wealthy stay wealthy by paying lower fees, charges and commissions. They buy only what they need so their costs—commissions, fees, etc. are less. They don't use middle-people because they know product providers only use their firms' high-cost products. Studies show:

> **"In every single time period and data point tested, low-cost funds beat high-cost funds."**
> http://www.cbsnews.com/news/morningstar-low-mutual-fund-fees-trump-our-star-ratings/

We follow investment legend, Benjamin Graham's advice and buy financial products like we buy "groceries, … not perfume." We use only the products best for us; not for the seller. Our edge is the miracle of compounding. As Warren Buffett said:

> "My wealth has come from a combination of living in America, some lucky genes, and **compound interest**."

Compounding your earnings *without fees or taxes* is the key.

Monthly	Accumulation at 12% per year									
	5	10	15	20	25	30	35	40	45	50
$100	$8,167	$23,004	$49,958	$98,925	$187,884	$349,496	$643,095	$1,176,477	$2,145,469	$3,905,834
$200	$16,334	$46,008	$99,916	$197,850	$375,768	$698,992	$1,286,190	$2,352,954	$4,290,938	$7,811,668
$300	$24,501	$69,012	$149,874	$296,775	$563,652	$1,048,488	$1,929,285	$3,529,431	$6,436,408	$11,717,502
$500	$40,835	$115,020	$249,790	$494,625	$939,420	$1,747,480	$3,215,475	$5,882,385	$10,727,346	$19,529,169

Warren Buffett does not "play" Wall Street's game. He **holds** the stocks of high-earning companies we use every day—Coke, GEICO, Fruit of the Loom, Benjamin Moore, Heinz, Burlington Northern, Dairy Queen, etc. berkshirehathaway.com/. He earns about 20% a year on average. We can earn 10-12% over time.

The **best guarantee of lifelong security is having money**. After we build a fund of $1,000,000, we can take $80,000 a year tax-FREE without running out of money for the rest of our lives. We need to think of investing as a business. We are building a business as a silent partner. We don't sell our assets just because our firms had a bad day or month or even year. American companies continue to grow by selling around the world. Many earn half their revenues from outside the U.S.

We **buy and hold the shares**—reinvesting the dividends automatically. We don't pay taxes every year on our dividends, stock splits and market gains: NO tax on gains ever. We don't panic and sell when the market falls. We own shares of many companies so our account will grow over time as America grows.

Our special account allows us to take out our **contributions** to pay for large purchases and deductibles. We avoid paying interest. It does not reduce our child's eligibility for school grants. Larger claims are paid by policies like HD-HSA plans. See chapter 10.

Our account will also cover our retirement income needs. We avoid the <u>tax on our Social Security benefits</u> too. We add an extra 50% to our nest egg. Our strategy helps us with higher retirement income for longer. All is tax-FREE and high-fee FREE.

We let compounding work its miracle over time. Our *Wealth Reserve*™ has more for later. We create our own guaranteed retirement supplement, long-term care insurance, and legacy all in one fund. We protect our future with *growing* assets. And the account is <u>protected from creditors in bankruptcy</u>.

Your first decision is where are you going to get the money to invest? I show you how to buy financial services directly from manufacturers. We buy value—**quality at the right price**. Today you can start keeping those extra premiums. You can accumulate that $175,000 instead of your insurer keeping it. You buy only what you need from quality companies at a discount. You can save $3,000 every year. You redirect it to your own account. You don't have to be wealthy or a financial genius to become financially independent. Your financial decisions provide cash.

You will handle every financial emergency with cash or with insurance that converts to cash. You can now guide your spending. You will have a **strategy** for investing, maintaining your lifestyle, and taking care of emergencies. You start by reviewing your coverages. Next you begin investing. It takes only an hour to set up our Simple, Easy and Wise Plan. You can 'manage' your tax-FREE *Wealth Reserve*™ in an hour a year. You don't pick stocks or chase yield. We let compounding work its miracle for us.

Once you are comfortable with your strategy, you have **patience**. You don't fear change. You understand it takes time for your "businesses" grow. You don't panic because you own the right kind of insurance. You have power for emergencies.

The *Wealth Reserve*™ is the best way to use **the power of compounding**—providing tax-FREE low-cost growth and income.

1

Create a tax-FREE investment account

In 322 B.C., Aristotle wrote:

'Money' is a guarantee that we may have what we want in the future. Though we need nothing at the moment, it insures the possibility of satisfying a necessary desire when it arises.

You are probably thinking this is a scam—how can I accumulate $100,000, let alone $1 million? How come I haven't heard about this before? Unfortunately our schools don't teach 'Compounding.'

Our schools teach banking. We all know how little our savings grows when we put it in a bank—0.1% to 1%. Then, every year, we are forced to pay taxes. This is why many people don't save! The accumulation doesn't look like it is worth giving up the things they want today for wealth tomorrow. It seems like that feeling is right! The bank does NOT compound high earnings.

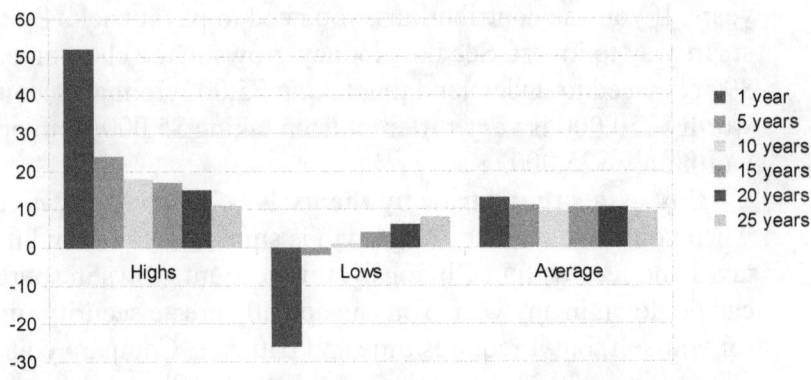

There is only one way for most of us to accumulate $1,000,000 from monthly contributions: We must buy and hold the securities of growing worldwide companies AND pay **zero** tax on the growth to maximize compounding. Yes, it is more likely that investing in growing company stocks can provide more wealth than gold, real estate, or get-rich-quick schemes. In fact, over most 10-year periods, there is **no safer investment than stocks**. Since few of us can actually pick, let alone invent the next "Apple," we must buy shares of a number of growing companies. If we buy a bunch using mutual funds, we have a good chance of earning 10% to 12% per year. We can ride out the 1 out of 500 possible company failures.

Compounding high earnings is key. The rich get richer—the top 1% take 23.5% of all income (up from 8.9%). And, as many millionaires have said, "the first million is the hardest." If you start with $3,000, it will take you 26 years of investing $3,000 a year in stocks to reach $500,000. (And only in a tax-FREE account.) However, when you have a HALF a million dollars, you only have to double your money to reach $1 million. Investors in stock funds, earning 10-12% on average, do this in 7-9 years without adding new money. Plus, the wealthy have found ways to pay less tax than we do. As Warren Buffett, with $54 Thousand Millions, admitted, "I pay at a lower overall tax rate than all of my office employees." He pays only 17% **total** tax—they pay 33%. Listen and weep: http://www.youtube.com/watch?v=Cu5B-2LoC4s.

You can create a **Wealth Reserve**™ of HALF a million by investing $250 a month because you are compounding at 10-12% over 26 years and you are not paying tax on the earnings. This plan also allows you to take out your contributions tax-FREE. If you let your money accumulate, you will have $1,000,000 in about 33 years. If you use contributions, you need to pay it back. That is the smart way to invest. See how money grows in the chart on page 39. You need to understand that taking $5,000 from an account worth $250,000 is **very** different from taking $5,000 from one worth only $25,000.

Buy assets that "grow by themselves." Money grows easily when you leave it alone. Its growth is stunted if you spend it or pay taxes and fees with it. Obviously, this account grows in spurts and can go down in any year. You can actually create security (money) for yourself, but it requires time and patience. Compare your bank CD earning .1%-2%. A bank account earning 2% while the inflation rate is 3% means that you are actually losing money (security) over time. Your $250-per-month deposit in the bank for 26 years will be worth about $105,000 after tax compared with about $500,000 in stock funds. Of course, since there is no tax due with a **Wealth Reserve**™ when you take the money out, you will be ecstatic every April 15 (tax time).

You will have security because your ***purchasing power*** has grown over time. If you doubt that the wealthy invest in the stock market for security, take a look at the long-term returns for various Vanguard mutual funds where they put their money. Some of these funds have provided investors with $2,000,000 or more for their retirement.

You might take a "loan" from your **Wealth Reserve**™ to buy your first home or for living expenses if you become disabled. Think of the security you have as you go through life. The **Wealth Reserve**™ that you have might launch you in a business or make sure your kids go to college. When you understand how your **Wealth Reserve**™ works, you will pay back the "loan" so you have the Reserve for another time. This is the lesson that the wealthy have learned generation after generation. You earn 10% to 12% on your money. You could buy all ten Vanguard funds and receive 11.5% total return after fees with less risk. When one fund is down, others are up.

2015 Total Return	Fund	Long-term Return	Longevity
1.4%	500 Index	10.8%*	since 1976
-21.5%	Energy	10.3%	since 1984
-3.3%	Extended Market Idx	10.6%	since 1987
12.7%	Health	17.3%	since 1984
-0.7%	International Growth	10.3%	since 1981
2.6%	PRIMECAP	13.5%	since 1984
-3.6%	Small Cap Index	10.5%	since 1960
1.3%	Wellesley Income	9.9%	since 1970
-3.3%	Windsor	11.3%	since 1958
-3.2%	Windsor II	10.6%	since 1985
-1.7%	Average	11.5%	

*Average Annual Returns as of 12/31/15.

That kind of security begins with your commitment to a regular contribution ... and patience. TIME will work magic on your **Wealth Reserve**™ fund. I was inspired by the patience of Susan and Fred, friends from work. Their financial plan was the inspiration for the "**Wealth Reserve**™." Here is their story:

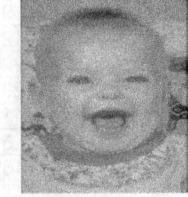

"Fred and Susan had a baby—Natalie—in 1975. They lived in lower Manhattan and I knew them because Susan worked with me sometimes. It began when we started talking about the baby. Susan asked me what to do with the money they received from relatives and friends for Natalie's birth. They wanted to protect their new child's future and to have college money. Both of them had good insurance benefits at work. I suggested that Susan and Fred look at individual stocks."

Susan and Fred's 'college" fund

Market Returns	Account Value	Natalie	Year	
	$5,000	Natalie		
37%	$12,604	0	1975	
24%	$20,837	1	1976	
-8%	$23,034	2	1977	
6%	$28,868	3	1978	
18%	$38,020	4	1979	Paid $1,000 to repair car
32%	$55,731	5	1980	
-5%	$56,934	6	1981	
22%	$74,584	7	1982	
21%	$95,328	8	1983	
6%	$105,500	9	1984	
32%	$129,804	10	1985	Paid $15000 for house
19%	$159,465	11	1986	
5%	$171,848	12	1987	
17%	$205,976	13	1988	
32%	$277,433	14	1989	
-3%	$273,184	15	1990	
31%	$363,373	16	1991	
8%	$396,979	17	1992	
10%	$441,296	18	1993	
2%	$454,406	19	1994	
38%	$632,877	20	1995	Susan disabled- stop $350/mo
23%	$772,138	21	1996	Paid $6,300 for vacation
33%	$970,594	22	1997	Paid $56,350 for loans and tax
28%	$1,232,360	23	1998	Paid $10,000 for roof repair
21%	$1,491,156	24	1999	
-9%	$1,356,952	25	2000	
-12%	$1,195,475	26	2001	
-22%	$931,275	27	2002	
29%	$1,201,344	28	2003	
11%	$1,333,492	29	2004	
5%	$1,400,167	30	2005	
16%	$1,624,194	31	2006	

*They contributed $350 per month or $4,200 per year to "college" fund. Inflation adjusted dollars.

"They talked it over and agreed. They asked me what stocks to buy and why. I told them they could pick any stock in the Dow. They picked the ones with the highest yield and the lowest price. Susan is bright. She was an underwriter. This was in 1975 or '76. I forget which ones they purchased—ATT, Johnson & Johnson, GE, GM—you know, the household names."

"They agreed on buying stocks because they could buy them directly from the companies and hold them without paying tax on the increased value until they needed the money. Dividends were reinvested and the income tax on the earnings was not outrageous. These plans are now called DSP and DRIPS. Susan and Fred called these accounts their "college fund." I think they had $5,000 from gifts and they contributed $350 a month ($6 a day) plus extra income from time to time. Most of the companies they picked allowed them to buy stocks without a broker's fee. By the time Natalie was 18, Fred and Susan had about $300,000."

"They kept putting money in each month. During the bad years—you know 1977-78, they had second thoughts. But Susan kept them on track."

"They had a car accident a few years after they started and needed money to pay for the policy deductible. They were saving about $200 a year by taking the $1,000 deductible. So they needed to sell $1,000 of stock. They sold stock that was down that year. In fact, I think they did not have to pay any tax on that sale. Anyway, that $1,000 sale did not hurt them. They still ended up with about $300,000. And remember, all this time—18 years—they have saved $200 on their car insurance. That's $3,600 of the $75,600 ($350 X 12 mo. X 18 yrs.) they invested."

"Like most families, they wanted a house. They got tired of paying rent and needed a good place for Natalie to go to school. The cost of the down payment—$15,000—came from Natalie's college fund. They still ended up with about $300,000. But what they found was that some of the stocks had done worse than others. They sold the worst ones, paying little tax on the gain. They found that most of the $15,000 withdrawal was money they had already paid tax on. They paid the capital gains tax of 20% on about $5,000 of the $15,000. That was the profit on the stock they sold."

"They usually receive a tax refund because they both worked, so that year it was smaller. That was all that happened. They purchased the house with the $15,000 and avoided the mortgage insurance that bankers usually charge those who have less than a 20% down payment. This saved them more money each year too."

"In a sense then, part of the $350 they paid each month for the college fund was actually paid for by the savings from the fact they had enough of a down payment not to need private mortgage insurance. They saved on their homeowners by picking a $5,000 deductible and not needing expensive extras, like coverage for jewelry or furs. They saved on credit life, disability, unemployment, and PMI insurance that the mortgage bank tried to add to their mortgage payment. All these helped pay for the college fund."

> Their "College" Fund became a **WEALTH RESERVE**

"No one explains these options when you are starting out. The agent wants to pile on more premiums to raise the commission. The banker wants to pile on higher mortgage fees. The lawyer doesn't get paid to save you money. Your parents help you as much as they can. Susan and Fred were lucky. They got the help they needed early, but everyone can do the same kind of saving today.

"In order to protect the $300,000 fund and all their other assets, Fred found out about umbrella liability insurance. For $210 a year, Susan and Fred would have $1,000,000 coverage in case they were sued and needed to pay a lawyer to defend themselves. Even if the accident was their fault, the policy covered the judgment and the lawyer fees too."

"They were finally ready for Natalie to go to college. They had $300,000 available for her when she was 18 years old. Of course she didn't need the money all at once. And when she made her decision about where to go to college she chose a very good state college that cost only $10,000 a year."

"During this time educational loans were very cheap. So Fred and Susan decided to let the college fund grow—20% to 25% a year—during the 90's. They knew this was unusual because the average gain for Dow stocks was 12% a year. They let the loans grow for the first two years until they could see that they had earned $60,000 for two years straight. We discussed this and decided this couldn't last. So they sold enough stock to pay the loans and the tax on the stock earnings. Now they realized they did not have to worry about the college loans any more."

"Susan told me right before she took another job that they had easily taken care of Natalie's college expense each year from the college fund. They stopped paying for life insurance policies that she and Fred owned. This saved them another $2,500 a year and they continued to invest the $350 per month. It was getting easier with fewer expenses. As a backup emergency fund, they took out a home equity line of credit that cost them nothing—no fees or closing costs. They would pay the loan market rate only *if* they needed to use the line for emergencies."

"One thing they did not anticipate: Susan was disabled within the year. She no longer had disability insurance from work. She was not able to work at all. They decided to cut back on their entertainment, vacation, and hobbies in order to get by on Fred's salary. They also had an emergency expense. They had to sell stock to pay $10,000 for Fred's parent's home repair. The tax on the earnings of the stocks did not push them into the next tax bracket, so they are actually paying much less tax this year anyway. Susan got better and they were able to give Natalie a fabulous graduation party and trip to California as a present."

"The next year after Natalie graduated; Susan and Fred decided to start their own business. Fred would work part-time. Susan would work full-time in what she loved—framing people's pictures. Fred would do the woodwork. Susan would run the store in a charming village nearby. The college fund—now $600,000 or so—gave them the feeling that they would have incomes until they got the store into the black. They paid the store's rent and utilities. The store liability policy was not too bad after Susan picked a higher deductible. Fred's job would provide the health insurance they needed."

> **WEALTH RESERVE** also used to self-insure some risks.

"The store business allows Fred and Susan to deduct many of the normal expenses associated with their activities. The 'college' fund, no longer for college, allowed them to save more on the protection they need for retirement. They attended a seminar on long term care insurance and decided that they could afford it but didn't need it. According to page 6 of the *Shopper's Guide* they received at the seminar, the chance of Fred needing expensive care was 4%; Susan 13%." [See our Insider's Guide to Long-term Care

Insurance at www.TheInsidersGuides.com]
"If they spent $4,000 a year for up to 30 years, they might never get to use that $120,000 [$2,000 each, times 30 years] because they both were in good health. Besides, 50% of LTCi buyers drop it before benefits begin. So, Fred and Susan put the $4,000 in their tax-advantaged retirement plan, connected with their business. This will add another $600,000 for any emergency, including remodeling their home for easy access and hiring a home health aide. These are the most common needs people have, according to the booklet. Worst case, they use the assets in the business which helps them with health care."

"Fred was still a teacher working part-time and Susan loves the way a picture looks—even bad ones—in a frame."

How the **Wealth Reserve**™ works

The **Wealth Reserve**™ is actually a Roth IRA or Roth 401k account—the IRS's own tax haven for the working person! The rules are pretty simple—taxed money goes in and tax-FREE earnings come out after age 59 ½. Borrow your contributions out anytime.

IRA contributions are limited to $5,500 (2013), but may rise in future years. There are income limits but most people don't hit the earnings limit of $127,000 (2013) until later. If we are married, the limit is $188,000 (2013). We make our deposit to our **Wealth Reserve**™ automatic so we can't forget to do it each month.

You may also invest in your employer's Roth 401k if your employer matches it. You don't reduce your income tax with these contributions. However, they grow tax FREE forever. You can contribute up to $17,500 (2013). If your employer matches your funds, it really boosts your 401k growth. **It's free money**. You will have tax-FREE income from both accounts later.

Of course you can make contributions to your Roth 401k if your employer offers low-cost funds. Many young people prefer to be taxed at the beginning of their careers since their salaries do not draw high tax rates yet. The contribution limit may be raised in the future: irs.gov/retirement/article/0,,id=152956,00.html#5.

There are no limits on an employee's income in determining if he or she can make designated Roth 401(k) contributions. Of course, the employer has to offer Roth 401(k) deferrals. If you decide to invest $10,000 a year for 24 years in a low-cost stock index fund inside their employer's Roth 401k plan, you could accumulate $1 million with NO federal income taxation to pay on the earnings. The tax savings might be worth an extra 30% since your federal and state tax payments are avoided.

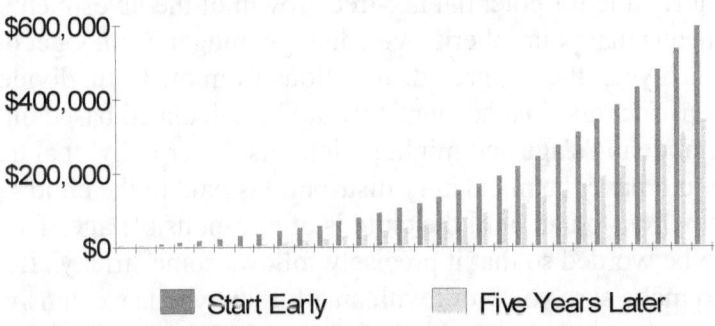

You can open your Roth IRA account at any age as long as you have *earned* income. Stock dividends or interest do not count. Any job will do. You don't even need a job requiring a W-2 to prove it. A part-time, weekend or night job will do. Any cash-only work will also qualify. Accountants recommend that receipts and records be maintained. You could even work for yourself in a home-office business.

Your contributions to the account should not pass through your hands to ensure success. You should have the money taken directly from your bank account by the IRA trustee. A Roth IRA must have existed for at least five years before you can borrow contributions. Contributions are after-tax so you can take them, if necessary, with no tax payable. Nontaxable distributions from a Roth IRA won't affect your eligibility for student aid either. Later, in retirement, this money won't affect your social security benefits as of the rules today.

Alternatively, if you already have a Roth IRA with significant values, you can use it to do your gift and estate planning. You don't have to take the money out beginning at age 70½, unlike the regular IRA. You can let it grow. You can name your grandchild beneficiary which will be effective for both property law and income tax purposes. Obviously, as beneficiary, your grandchild could just liquidate the account and thus lose the value for their

"Gift of a Lifetime." If you fear this could happen, you could name your child or you might need to establish a trust to control the distributions. See your lawyer.

A person who inherits a Roth—unlike the original owner of the account—is required to withdraw a percentage of the funds annually, based on their age. The younger the person when they inherit, the longer they can stretch out those withdrawals, enjoying more time for potential tax-free growth of the investments. That means that your inheritance could get bigger as they get older. Each year, the required distributions from the Roth, divided into separate inherited accounts, would be calculated based on each grandchild's age and might go into his or her individual trust. You could have the mandatory distributions paid to the child's parent or other custodian until the child is of a responsible age. The trust has to be worded so that it precisely follows some "tricky" IRS rules, so make sure you work with an attorney who has extensive experience setting these up. A $100,000 inherited Roth IRA could be worth $2-3 millions over their lifetimes.
http://www.fairmark.com/rothira/inherit.htm

If you own a Roth IRA, you can split it into equal shares and name each grandchild as primary beneficiary. While the Roth IRAs will be included in your taxable estate and so be subject to federal estate tax, the Roth IRA will pass to the grandchild and could be tax free. This is not tax advice. See your lawyer.

Your grandchildren can avoid the 10% early distribution penalty and withdraw earnings tax-FREE even if they are under age 59½. They inherited the money. Usually the grandchild can take distributions over their entire life span—reducing the amount and allowing the bulk of the inheritance to grow tax-FREE. Ask your accountant for details.

The Roth IRA is NOT the best way for you to save for your kid's college expenses. You can own a 529 college savings plan for the benefit of your child. You can contribute more money to a 529 than to a Roth IRA. Grandparents can lower their estate tax by contributing. You can change beneficiaries if your child does not want to go to college. You can use it yourself. You don't give up control of the funds. And if started early enough, 18 years is enough time to accumulate completely tax-FREE funds (including earnings) for education expenses. Find our Insiders Guide to Education Funding through TheInsidersGuides.com

The Roth IRA allows you take "qualified" withdrawals—for your 1st home and disability—which are not included as taxable income, unlike other savings plans—savings bonds, mutual funds, etc. You benefit through lower income taxes by putting money in a tax-free investment versus paying taxes on dividends each year in a taxable savings or investment account.

The miracle of compounding and tax-FREE growth

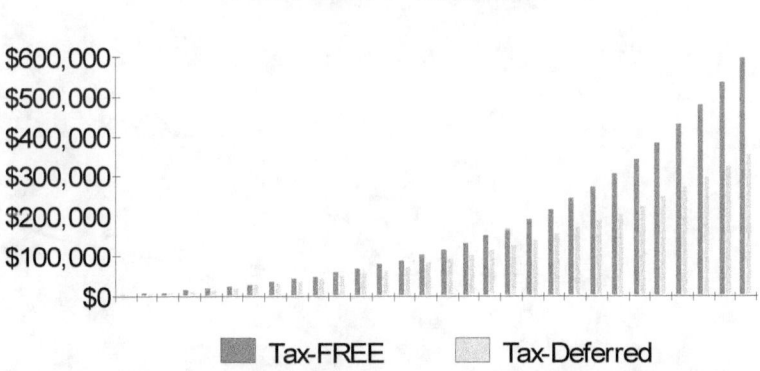

Ben Franklin was wrong about death and taxes! Taxes can be avoided. The point of your contributions to a Roth IRA is that the growth of the contributions is NOT TAXED as it grows and NOT TAXED as it comes out of the account.

No other investment vehicle is like that. Your **Wealth Reserve**™ balloons to $1,000,000 because 1) it grows without taxation, and 2) time allows interest to be earned on interest and earnings on earnings. The account grows in **geometric progression**. The top lines in the graph below is measured on a larger scale than the bottom ones. Since the money is invested in stocks over a long period of time, it can compound at 10% to 12% annually, assuming you don't take touch it.

Using both of these factors creates a balance that really *sings*. Taken individually by themselves, your monthly contributions of any amount might not impress you. However, time—compounding —and tax-FREE earnings really gets your attention over the years. This is how wealth is created. A wealthy person works the same number of days as you do. However, when their wealth works day and night too, the accumulation line (top lines) can literally go off the chart. In most 10-year periods, losses are recovered.

Cumulative Wealth

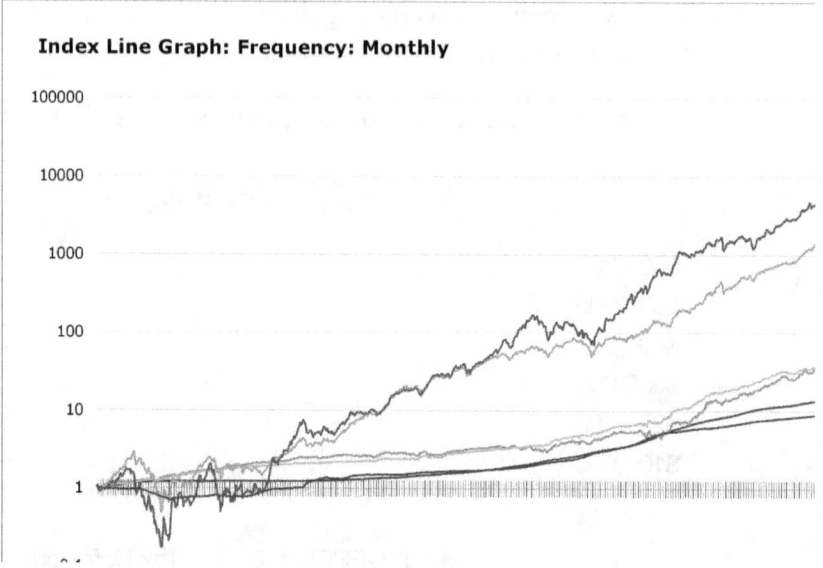

Top line—Small Cap Stocks
2nd line—Large Cap Stocks (S&P 500)
3rd line—US Long-term Corporate Bonds
4th line—Intermediate-term Government Bonds
5th line—US 30 day Government T-bills
6th line—US inflation

Courtesy: Dr. Campbell R. Harvey http://www.duke.edu/~charvey/

Historically, wealth doubles in value every 7-10 years if left alone. Of course the stock market doesn't move up at 10% every year. However, the **Wealth Reserve**™ will double and double and double so that by age 65, you could have over $1 million. Notice how the account values in the graph on page 39 move from $1 million to $2 million in 9 years, even with 3 years of losses. Of course, a million dollars will be worth less in the future because of inflation. But you will certainly appreciate your account later no matter what your contributions are now.

And the bonus of this geometric account growth is that it does not quit even if you stop adding your monthly contributions. Once the account has reached a certain mass, let's say after 30 years of contributions or $90,000, it will keep compounding. On page 39 we show you how this can work for contributions to a **Wealth Reserve**™ invested in an actual U.S. stock index fund (500 Index) over time.

You can see in the chart "Cumulative Wealth" above that over time, wealth accumulates at different rates depending on the type of assets you buy. For anyone who invested in smaller companies over any given 15 year period, the benefits were outstanding. For each $1,000 invested in 1940, $3,000,000 was the total return by the 1990's. Investing more cautiously, in the large companies of the S&P 500, for instance, your $1,000 would have grown to almost a $1,000,00 by 2000. Yes, the lines are not perfectly straight, but growing $250 a month to $1,000,000 is definitely worth the ups and downs. Inflation is designated by the bottom line here. Putting all your money in a bank CD would accumulate at a rate represented by a line near that bottom line.

You can see that the **best gift you can give to yourself** is a **Wealth Reserve**™ invested in a group of stocks over a long period of time. A low-cost index fund like the Vanguard Total Stock Index provides the best chance of maximizing earnings as the market leaders change over time. It won't matter which style or sector is rising or falling at any given time. The account owns them all and thus you benefit over the long haul. Since stocks have averaged about 10% over time and an index costs only 0.07% ($7 per $10,000), your account compounds at 10% or more versus 8.5% for funds paying managers with expensive bonuses. Vanugard has no owners to keep your fees. According to a Morningstar study:

> **"In every single time period and data point tested, low-cost funds beat high-cost funds."**
>   personal.vanguard.com/pdf/morningstar.pdf

You can understand how this account works. If you don't stop contributing or take money out when the account goes down temporarily, you will have money for retirement. Learn patience. TIME is the key ingredient in this formula. Success does not require stock trading. Get-rich-quick schemes only work for the seller. This plan does not require working longer hours. It does not require checking your account every day. **It requires just waiting** for compounding to work. And sometimes that is hard to do. When others panic, you must be steady. Start it and forget it.

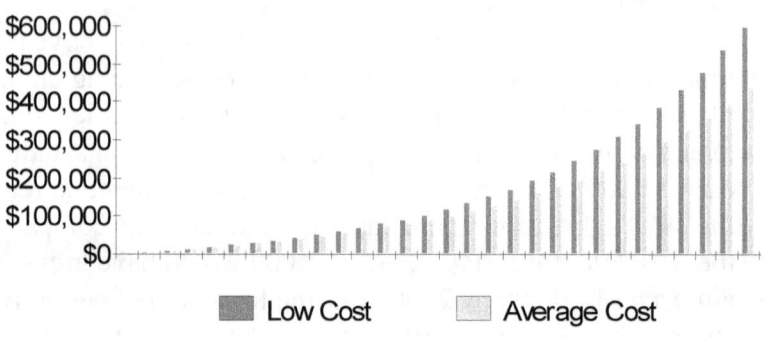

How to get started

All you have to do is open the account online or by phone, provide a bank account number to the trustee and sign the paperwork. Do it and forget it. Licensed advisors replace your salesperson and answer your questions. The Gift of a Lifetime takes an hour.

Let's say you don't have $250 a month. Of course, you can invest whatever you want. But you want to help yourself as much as possible. You can use our *Guides* to uncover savings in your current spending that can provide money for your contributions. You can use our *Guides* to redirect premiums and fees to your **Wealth Reserve**™ for *your* future instead of theirs.

For instance, you could save $600 or more just by changing your deductible on your auto or home insurance. Learn the insider tricks of buying auto and home coverage and save. See **Insider's Guides to Vehicle** and **Home Insurance** below. You might drop some of the coverage you don't need, like credit or permanent life insurance. Check our **Insider's Guide to Buying Life Insurance**. You could save big by transferring your mutual funds to a low-cost provider like Vanguard or TIAA which are not for profit. Some clients have saved $3,000 a year just with this one change. You will discover that no money manager can be right all the time. Market index funds beat 86% of all managed mutual funds. Use our **Insider's Guide to Buying Mutual Funds & Securities**. businessweek.com/investing/insights/blog/archives/2009/04/

If you are like most people, you want to save on the things you really don't need but you don't know which financial products are best or where to buy them. Many people can save $3,000 a year without changing their lifestyles. Often, it is just a matter of recognizing that we have changed but our old obligations have not. We don't examine our habits. For instance, some people find their cable bill has escalated and they really don't need a package they still have. Others don't realize they don't need life and disability insurance in their auto policy. The routines of daily life don't let us question our assumptions periodically. Family needs and lifestyles change. We become involved in different activities. We just don't question what we spend money on.

You can also help yourself by using our *Guides* when you need any financial product. When it comes time to buy a mortgage or invest for college, let our *Guides* help you decide which account is best. You could save on banking and auto purchases. Our *Guide* offers insider advice from those who work in these industries.

Our *Guides* show you how to buy only what you need, not what provides the highest profit to the sellers. After working in the financial services business for 20 years—brokerage, banks, advisory firm—I can assure you that the retail products offered to the public are created and chosen for the benefit of the sellers not the end user—you. This industry has changed dramatically. Now you can buy and sell stocks for zero commission, invest in a mutual fund for fees of 0.01%, buy term life insurance directly for 60% off retail. You can buy almost all financial products at substantial discounts from the products sold by the industry middle-people. The products are usually better too.

> **WEALTH RESERVE** provides tax-FREE income

So you can help yourself by building your **Wealth Reserve**™ of $1 million AND finding how and where to save on all your financial needs. Take advantage of these savings too. Add them to your Reserve: See the list of savings below. The *Guides* are now available in one volume at TheInsidersGuides.com.

Now you have a plan to build a **Wealth Reserve**™. It can serve as your **emergency** fund, your **self-insurance** fund, your **loan** fund, and your **retirement** system. Over your lifetime, you have a way to meet your needs without wasting money on taxes, fees and interest paid to others. You are using your money to buy assets that "grow by themselves." Your money pays *you* interest instead of you paying interest to others. Your account compounds capital gains on capital gains. None of it is used to pay taxes.

Hear how Earl Crawley did it: http://www.youtube.com/watch?v=XD0svDGyLWU

You have the **new financial system**. It doesn't matter what happens to Social Security or your company's pension plan. You are *not* relying on the government or others to pay or not pay toward your bountiful lifestyle.

You invest $99,000 ($3,000 a year 33 years) for $1,000,000.

Your **Wealth Reserve**™ is your new financial system

Monthly	Accumulation at 12% per year									
	5	10	15	20	25	30	35	40	45	50
$100	$8,167	$23,004	$49,958	$98,925	$187,884	$349,496	$643,095	$1,176,477	$2,145,469	$3,905,834
$200	$16,334	$46,008	$99,916	$197,850	$375,768	$698,992	$1,286,190	$2,352,954	$4,290,938	$7,811,668
$300	$24,501	$69,012	$149,874	$296,775	$563,652	$1,048,488	$1,929,285	$3,529,431	$6,436,408	$11,717,502
$500	$40,835	$115,020	$249,790	$494,625	$939,420	$1,747,480	$3,215,475	$5,882,385	$10,727,346	$19,529,169

2

A Simple, Easy and Wise Plan

People who are successful have a plan.

If you want to have a $500,000 financial system, you need a way to make it happen. To be able to have a nest egg of $1 million by age 67 requires that you know how to start investing, invest regularly, invest properly, monitor accumulations along the way, and get help when you need it. It takes only one hour to set up the Simple, Easy and Wise Plan and only 1 hour per year to manage it.

Picking *individual* stocks as a strategy is not likely to work for you. Warren Buffett is probably history's greatest investor, in terms of results with $54 BILLION ($54 thousand million dollars) so far. He buys *companies* that provide valuable services to a great number of people. His company owns parts of Coke, GEICO, Fruit of the Loom, Benjamin Moore, Heinz, Burlington Northern, etc. berkshirehathaway.com/ He told Reuters: "A very low-cost index is going to beat a majority of the amateur-managed money or professionally-managed money." Many studies have shown that low-cost index funds beat 86% of funds with a stock picking manager. *BusinessWeek* Apr 2009. A February 2009 study provides more evidence that investing in simple, low-cost **index funds** often leads to better net returns. Compare the odds of selecting the correct mutual fund. Your fund's chance of beating the market in EACH year is 3 out of 100. nytimes.com/2009/02/22/your-money/stocks-and-bonds/22stra.html

Other studies have shown that successful investing is a result of owning quality stocks or stock mutual funds **over a long period of time**. Most people are not patient so they are not successful investors. You can build wealth by owning the stocks of profitable businesses over time. Anne Scheiber did it by herself and left $20 million to her favorite charity, money.cnn.com/magazines/moneymag/moneymag_archive/1996/01/01/207651/index.

I have helped people who have never reached their goal

because they have not learned what it takes to get there. They started saving but they did not learn about the **miracle of compounding.** They saved in their bank at 2% or 3% interest rate. They became frustrated because they only had $18,000 after three years of saving $500 a month. So they quit saving and bought a SuperCrew 145 XLT for $637 a month for 60 months. They did not know that they could have earned over $50,000 by investing that same amount of money in a low-cost stock mutual fund.

Most people never learn how compounding of earnings works. In short, we never learn that every $100 is worth $10,000 to you in time if you invest in companies that share their profits with you. A stock index fund helps you earn an average of 12% per year without losing all your money if one company fails. You cannot become financially independent without investing in profitable companies. Compare your actual returns from bank CDs to stocks. At 3%, your $250 monthly contribution to a CD earns $200,000 in 33 years. At 12%, your **Wealth Reserve**™ would have about $1 million from stocks. Which do you want?

A Simple, Easy, Wise Strategy

My strategy incorporates a unique technique to assure that you reach your goal: a **Wealth Reserve**™. People spend more time planning a vacation than their financial future. You can use a simple, easy and wise strategy to insure yourself of a healthy financial life. Consistency wins. You create a **Wealth Reserve**™ as Step 1.

> Start your **WEALTH RESERVE** in three steps

Step 1. Build your **Wealth Reserve**™. Your **Wealth Reserve**™ consists of mutual funds inside the Roth IRA trust account. The account grows without taxation on the earnings. You may also invest through a Roth 401k at work. Since few companies are offering a paid pension, most independents are making the investment decisions on their own. A **Wealth Reserve**™ refers to the fact that it can also be used to insure some of your risks. You are relieved of the need to waste money on some insurance policies. You are building a reserve against a possible loss and creating more Wealth at the same time. The Reserve may serve two purposes—a Reserve for unforeseen contingencies and a fund that makes loans and later provides income to supplement a modified Social Security.

A great example of this is the risk of premature death. With a term policy for 10 at a time, you can replace lost family income if you are not around. You can buy a 10 year term policy for about a $1 a day even at age 50. If you have built your **Wealth Reserve**™ over time, your family will have a **Wealth Reserve**™ of much more than a permanent life insurance benefit can possibly provide.

Before easy access to mutual funds, life insurance was considered an investment. If you paid $2,000 a year in premiums for 50 years, your family would receive a benefit of $300,000 at your death! Today, you and your family can enjoy $1 million for any lifestyle need! You can obtain term to cover your family for $1 a day during your working years. It is cheap because the risk is low. Your **Wealth Reserve**™ is there for you in case you are disabled or your Social Security is reduced. Your family will have money to make the transition if you are not around.

During your working life, you will earn about $2.5 to $3 million before taxes. If you invest **just** 10 percent of that income, you can accumulate another $1 million to accomplish all that you want to do in life. Your **Wealth Reserve**™ assures you of having enough no matter what happens. I assume that you will not spend every cent that you earn. However, if you start investing early, you will provide the reserve of $1 million when you need it. Investing is really about TIME. Consider what would have happened if your parents had invested $100 a month since your birth. Your **Wealth Reserve**™ might be $125,000 by now, depending on the asset they bought. You might have $1 million by age 40.

How assets build the **Wealth Reserve**™

Monthly	Accumulation at 12% per year									
	5	10	15	20	25	30	35	40	45	50
$100	$8,167	$23,004	$49,958	$98,925	$187,884	$349,496	$643,095	$1,176,477	$2,145,469	$3,905,834
$200	$16,334	$46,008	$99,916	$197,850	$375,768	$698,992	$1,286,190	$2,352,954	$4,290,938	$7,811,668
$300	$24,501	$69,012	$149,874	$296,775	$563,652	$1,048,488	$1,929,285	$3,529,431	$6,436,408	$11,717,502
$500	$40,835	$115,020	$249,790	$494,625	$939,420	$1,747,480	$3,215,475	$5,882,385	$10,727,346	$19,529,169

It is never too late. Start today

Step **2**. The *amount of time* you have to accomplish your goal determines the type of investment you need. Even though we can't predict the day, month and year of ups and downs, the stock market goes up about 10-12% a year, over most 10-year periods. These Vanguard mutual funds have earned over 10% after fees for a long time. Of course, there is no guarantee of future returns:

2014 Total Return	Fund	Long-term Return	Longevity
13.5%	500 Index	11.1%*	since 1976
-14.3%	Energy	11.5%	since 1984
7.4%	Extended Market Idx	11.1%	since 1987
28.5%	Health	17.4%	since 1984
-5.6%	International Growth	10.6%	since 1981
18.7%	PRIMECAP	13.9%	since 1984
7.5%	Small Cap Index	9.3%	since 1960
8.1%	Wellesley Income	10.1%	since 1970
11.8%	Windsor	11.6%	since 1958
11.2%	Windsor II	11.1%	since 1985
8.7%	Average	11.8%	

*Average Annual Returns as of 12/31/14.

Most pension funds are invested in stocks and bonds. Even though the market fell 22% in 2002 and jumped 29% in 2003, the average was still holding. See page 39. And, with a Roth IRA, your money can compound tax-FREE, providing an extra 25% when you take it out. You never pay income tax.

Turn $3.33 into $1 million

It matters how much money you start investing with but the **key to reaching any money goal is TIME**—not luck or skill. You need TIME to let the power of compounding work its magic to turn even $3.33 a day into $1 million. The chart on page 29 illustrates how even a small amount—$3.33 a day ($100 per month)—can grow to over $1 million. Most people will need that $1 million later as our life expectancies grow to 90 years.

You can build a $1 million fund faster (25 years), but you need to invest $500 a month in a low-cost stock mutual fund. Since the Roth IRA contribution limit is now $5,500 and is expected to increase in step with inflation, you should have no problem building your **Wealth Reserve**™ over time. Try different numbers: moneychimp.com/articles/rothira/contribution_limits.htm

Step 3. **Start NOW**. It's never too late. $3.33 is affordable for everyone. Buy one or all 10 of the funds listed above. They are assets that *grow by themselves*. At $3.33 a day, $100 a month, you pay $46,800 for $1 million. If you are under age 30, you have time enough that your contributions can reach $1 million. You and your spouse might afford $6,000 a year to reach $1 million in less than 30 years. If you are a parent, you can give the Gift of a Lifetime to your child: just $10,000 invested by age 20 can become $1 million by age 67. moneychimp.com/calculator/compound_interest_calculator.htm

Most successful people let TIME do the work. As Warren Buffett, the world's best investor, said, "We continue to make more money when *snoring* than when active." Berkshirehathaway.com/

If your goal is to provide a college education and you can invest $3.33 a day for 18 years, you can have about $90,000 for their education. If you invest another $3.33 a day for 39 years, you could have over $1 million for your retirement. And using a ROTH IRA makes it tax-FREE. fairmark.com/rothira/contrib.htm

My clients implemented their strategy by calling one of the low-cost mutual funds like Vanguard, Fidelity or TIAA-CREF and opening a Roth IRA account. Others did it online. These firms provide the best value for your money since their fees are low.

Since they completed the application themselves, they saved 5.75% of their money on commissions (loads). Vanguard.com and TIAA-CREF.org are run for your benefit—not the managers—so their annual fees are very low—at cost.

You can request a ROTH IRA application by phone. You may have a tax penalty if use all of it before age 60. Exceptions: first home and disability See RothIRA.com. Compounding without current taxes supercharges your **Wealth Reserve**™. If you already have a Roth IRA, you can fund your spouse's, child's or grandchild's.

For each $50 we save, Uncle Sam "gives" us $19 in TAX-FREE gains.

A ROTH IRA allows you to grow the assets without tax ... ever —it's FREE of federal income tax as long as you keep it open for five years and withdraw earnings after age 59½, except for paying for your first home and disability income. Also, you may receive a tax CREDIT for $1,000 for your ROTH IRA (2013).

Request a prospectus (owner's manual) for each fund you will be using. Most clients favor low-cost. Your **Wealth Reserve**™ is a long-term investment, so buy one or more of the Vanguard funds above. Other low-cost funds are provided by TIAA-CREF Equity Index or the Fidelity Spartan. The Vanguard 500 has very large American companies. Some clients add International Stock or TIAA International Equity since they represent markets around the world. The Energy and Health funds already have global giants.

Keep it simple by buying all the funds from one company. You will receive only one statement with the fund's returns listed.

The account application allows you to begin an automatic monthly debit from your checking account. This assures that you pay the lowest share cost. There is a section for Roth IRA beneficiaries. Most people list their spouse as primary and children as contingent. The telephone representatives can answer any specific fund questions you have.

This strategy provides you with the **best chance of accumulating** the greatest amount with the least risk over time while not wasting a dime of your money on a high paid manager. You may use a Roth 401k at work if fees are low. Some plans have excessive costs (uselaws.com/news/3/124). That Roth 401k works the same way but you can contribute much more to it.
irs.gov/retirement/article/0,,id=152956,00.html.

The Simple Financial Life strategy provides you with diversification and "dollar cost averaging," the lowest-cost method (investopedia.com) of buying the companies you may use everyday. Pensions, insurers, and trusts invest in the market using low-cost funds just like you can. An advisor is not necessary since you are not interested in chasing last year's hot mutual fund. The expenses are as low as $7 per $10,000 vs. $134 every year for the average stock fund manager's high salary.

Why use funds from Vanguard or TIAA?

Did you know that most Wall Street insiders do not follow the advice of retail brokers or the popular financial press? They invest most of their serious money in low-cost funds or shares of index funds (ETFs) because they realize excessive costs lower the returns of most fund managers over 10 years, especially in down markets.

There are many books written on the subject of index versus "managed" funds. If you wish to vanquish the hype and understand investing, skim *A Random Walk Down Wall Street* by Princeton University's Burton Malkiel. Here are the reasons why smart insiders use low-cost funds:

1. Both stock and bond index funds provide better returns than 86% of managed funds for periods greater than 10 years.
2. You earn more because you pay lower costs and taxes.
3. Low-cost funds build greater wealth over time.
4. Low-cost funds can be less volatile because they reflect whole sectors of the market.
5. Low-cost funds offer better diversification.
6. You know what you are paying for. No high-salary managers.
7. Low-cost funds don't require you to hope the manager will predict the future correctly. The odds of doing it are 1 in 15,000 each year separately. Over time, all funds provide average returns minus their costs.
8. Low-cost funds are easy to buy.

> "Professional money management is a gigantic rip-off."
> Bill Gross, star bond manager, *Everything You've Heard About Investing is Wrong*

This is a summary of many studies about investing

First, fund managers try to predict the future of the market when they buy and sell securities in their funds. There is no proof this can be done well over time. Yesterday's winners are usually tomorrow's losers. The AVERAGE market return has been 12%, so a few managers will beat the average by luck—Just not the same ones every year. nytimes.com/2008/07/13/business/13stra.html

Second, the costs of the manager, their staff and operations must be paid for by you whether or not they earn you a dime. It is always better to pay as little as possible for the same performance. Costs can take 33% of your returns over time. Surprisingly, while

the stock index rose 9%, investors with high paid managers averaged only **3.79%** annually (QAIB). DALBARinc.com.
Third, high cost managers get paid for increasing the size of their funds, not for making you rich. Bringing in more money is a full-time job. It is expensive to market the funds given that there are now thousands available. It is inevitable that popular funds will grow until they produce average returns with high expenses. Managers want to be rich, not right.
Fourth, there is much less chance of you being treated poorly by fund management if the structure and governance are customer-oriented like Vanguard's and TIAA's are.
Fifth, many professional managers and Wall Street insiders place their core assets in low-cost index funds.

Here are some of their statements:

Warren Buffett, the most successful investor
"Most investors, both institutional and individual, will find that the best way to own common stocks is through an index fund that charges minimal fees.... Paradoxically, when 'dumb' money acknowledges its limitations, it ceases to be dumb." Berkshirehathaway.com/letters/1993.html.

Peter Lynch, brilliant manager, Magellan Fund "…you'd be just as well off if you'd invested in the S&P 500." *One Up on Wall Street*, 1989, p. 240.

Jonathan Clements, formerly ***The Wall Street Journal***
"Most people can do it themselves. ... By indexing, you don't just ensure that you will do better than most other investors. You will also enjoy the advantage of 'relative certainty.' . . . For most investors, Vanguard will be the place to go." *You've Lost It, Now What? How to beat the bear market and still retire on time*, 2003, p. 62, 70.

Charles D. Ellis, money managers' consultant
"The premise . . . that professional investment managers ***can*** beat the market . . . appears to be false. It is a loser's game. … clients would have done better in a market fund." Returns are "splendidly

predictable—on average and over time." *Investment Policy, How to Win the Loser's Game*, 1985, p. 5, 20, 34.

Jane Bryant Quinn, consumer advisor
"I'm a longtime booster of index mutual funds. These funds follow the market as a whole. Tons of research has shown that most money managers don't beat the markets they invest in, after costs. Maybe your own stocks or funds have excelled in the past couple of years. But in most cases, you've also been taking extra risk. The odds of superior performance are against you, in the long run. Indexing puts the odds on your side." *Los Angeles Business Journal*, May 8, 2000

Charles Schwab founder, discount broker
"I put my money where my mouth is: most of the mutual fund investments I have are in index funds, approximately 75%. My core investments are index funds. Experienced investors have discovered that in any given year, on average, only 20 to 30 percent of mutual funds outperform the market. That is why I recommend index funds…"
Mr. Schwab tells of one of his friends who owned many well-run funds. After keeping track of all the dividends, taxes, reinvestments tax basis and statements, he found he earned the same return as the index of these funds. After selling them all, he bought the index fund. He has "what he wanted in the first place: diversification, tax advantages, one statement, and lower expenses." *Guide to Financial Independence*, 1998, pp. 90, 103, 111.

Motley Fool, Internet site about investing
"Almost *everything* that you will ever read about mutual funds beyond, "Buy an index fund." is superfluous to your long-term success in investing in mutual funds." Fool.com.

Walter Updegrave, senior editor, *Money*
"Mutual fund picking would be easier if there was one you could count on to outperform 70% or so of its competitors over long stretches of a decade or more. It's called an index fund. Although less than 10% of investors own an index fund, they are "one of the best-kept secrets" on Wall Street. My unabashed aim is to convince you to put at least a part of your money into one or more of these

funds. You have a far less than a 50% chance of beating the market.... I strongly recommend that you make index funds your primary holding...." *The Right Way to Invest in Mutual Funds*, 1996, p 189-194.

Andrew Tobias, financial writer
"Scrimp and save, putting whatever you can into no-load, low-expense stock market index funds, both U.S. and foreign. You will do better than 80% of your friends and neighbors." *My Vast Fortune*, 1997, p. 158.

Vanguard and TIAA-CREF

The Masters of Index Funds, The Vanguard Group, is owned by its 18 million shareholders—NOT by a management company—holding over $1.4 trillion assets for institutions and individuals.

Vanguard offers no-load funds with the lowest operating expenses: $9 for each $10,000 compared with $205 per year for some funds. Over 40 years, your $10,000 index fund may grow to $931,000 versus $453,000 for a managed fund. Vanguard.com **800-252-9578** offers *Plain Talk* unbiased guides on many subjects. You can invest automatically from your bank account to your mutual fund account online. Apply online or phone: STAR minimum $1,000. Your strategy is Simple, Easy and Wise.

TIAA-CREF is the world's largest pension company, primarily for educational and research institutions. With $430 billion in assets, this organization now offers its low-cost products, with the highest service quality, to individuals too. TIAA holds the highest ratings from the four leading rating agencies. Low expenses and low initial contributions make TIAA an organization you can stay with for life.

At TIAA-CREF.org, you can make application and begin immediately with an automatic monthly contribution of $100 or more from their bank account. You can follow how the assets grow by themselves from your computer. This makes this strategy Simple, Easy and Wise.

Both firms are focused on *you*, not on manager profits.

Investing for the long-term (10+ years) creates wealth. But, it requires patience. Successful investors treat investing like a business. They have learned to control their emotions by using an investment policy statement. For financially-independent people, this is an important document.

Your investment policy can be as simple as enabling the automatic investment option on your application. If you begin by investing $250 a month in the Vanguard 500 Index or the TIAA Equity Index, you have your investment policy. You will not stop investing in that or other equity funds until you reach your goal. Your will continue the process without touching the money.

Increase returns and reduce risk using Modern Portfolio Theory

Some clients use the MPT strategy to control risk while increasing returns. Modern Portfolio Theory (Moneychimp.com/articles/risk/riskintro.htm) says that if you put your eggs in different baskets of assets that grow at different times, then the value of all your eggs grows with fewer ups and downs. You can manage the ups and downs of equity funds by buying and re-balancing different ones over time. Higher risk assets are small caps, REITs and foreign stocks. This strategy earns 10-12% with 30% less volatility.

Members assemble asset classes callan.com/research/download/?file=periodic/free/457.pdf
that fit their risk-reward tastes. According to this Nobel Prize-winning strategy moneychimp.com/articles/risk/portfolio.htm, a high return asset with a low correlation to other assets in the portfolio can actually reduce the risk of the whole. It may be possible to earn high returns with less risk **overall** as each asset goes up and down. See the example at fool.com/personal-finance/retirement/2007/03/06/5-steps-to-salvage-your-retirement.aspx.

Some clients use this strategy. Dimentional provides the benchmarks for comparisons. Dfaus.com Followers of MPT build a portfolio out of low-cost index funds or ETFs. Researchers found that small and value (high book-value-to-price ratio) stock funds have tended to do better than the market as a whole, but have greater volatility. When combined, volatility may be less.

The past provides only PROBABLE futures. But isn't $1,000,000 (plus or minus $100,000) better than $165,000. Your $250-per-month deposit in the bank for 33 years will be worth about $165,000 after tax compared with about $1 million from investing with no tax. Every child would be better off with $1 million (+/- $100,000) than $165,000 from a bank. Note the 2nd line versus the bottom line:

Cumulative Wealth

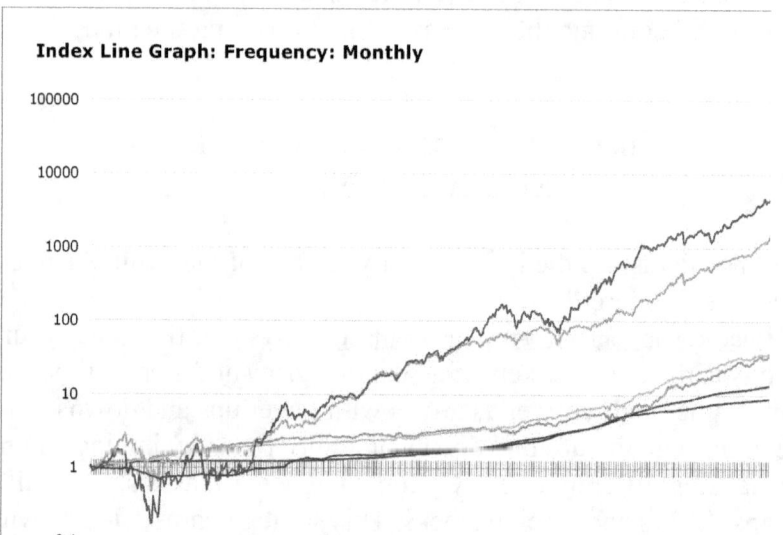

Top line—Small Cap Stocks
2nd line—Large Cap Stocks (S&P 500)
3rd line—US Long-term Corporate Bonds
4th line—Intermediate-term Government Bonds
5th line—US 30 day Government T-bills
6th line—US inflation

Courtesy Dr. Campbell R. Harvey http://www.duke.edu/~charvey/

$2,000 Annual Stock Market Investment 1950- '70- '80- '90- 2013

Year	Returns	Balance	Balance	Balance	Balance
		$2,000			
1950	31%	$2,620			
1951	24%	$5,729			
1952	18%	$9,120			
1953	-1%	$11,009			
1954	52%	$19,773			
1955	31%	$28,523			
1956	5%	$32,049			
1957	-11%	$30,304			
1958	43%	$46,194			
1959	12%	$53,978			
1960	1%	$56,538			
1961	26%	$73,757			
1962	-8%	$69,697			
1963	24%	$88,904			
1964	16%	$105,449			
1965	12%	$120,342			
1966	-10%	$110,108			
1967	24%	$139,014			
1968	11%	$156,526			
1969	-8%	$145,844	2,000		
1970	4%	$153,757	2,080		
1971	14%	$177,563	4,651		
1972	19%	$213,681	7,915		
1973	-14%	$185,485	8,527		
1974	-26%	$138,739	7,790		
1975	37%	$192,813	13,412		
1976	24%	$241,568	19,111		
1977	-8%	$224,082	19,422		
1978	6%	$239,647	22,707		
1979	18%	$285,144	29,155	2,000	
1980	32%	$379,030	41,124	2,640	
1981	-5%	$361,978	40,968	4,408	
1982	22%	$444,053	52,421	7,818	
1983	21%	$539,724	65,850	11,879	
1984	6%	$574,228	71,921	14,712	
1985	32%	$760,621	97,575	22,060	
1986	19%	$907,519	118,494	28,632	
1987	5%	$954,995	126,519	32,163	
1988	17%	$1,119,684	150,367	39,971	
1989	32%	$1,480,623	201,125	55,402	2,000
1990	-3%	$1,438,144	197,031	55,680	1,940
1991	31%	$1,886,589	260,731	75,560	5,161
1992	8%	$2,039,676	283,749	83,765	7,734
1993	10%	$2,245,843	314,324	94,342	10,708
1994	2%	$2,292,800	322,651	98,268	12,962
1995	38%	$3,166,824	448,018	138,370	20,647
1996	23%	$3,897,654	553,522	172,656	27,856
1997	33%	$5,186,540	738,844	232,292	39,709
1998	28%	$6,641,331	948,281	299,894	53,387
1999	21%	$8,038,430	1,149,839	365,291	67,019
2000	-9%	$7,316,791	1,048,174	334,235	62,807
2001	-12%	$6,447,855	925,203	296,223	57,095
2002	-22%	$5,024,437	722,291	232,316	46,035
2003	29%	$6,459,474	930,787	301,119	61,730
2004	11%	$7,164,483	1,034,274	336,099	70,664
2005	5%	$7,512,677	1,084,540	352,433	74,098
2006	15%	$8,694,884	1,259,259	412,409	90,450
2007	5%	$9,163,538	1,327,133	434,638	95,325
2008	-39%	$5,601,431	813,388	268,074	60,754
2009	27%	$7,116,358	952,155	342,993	79,699
2010	15%	$8,186,112	1,097,278	396,742	93,954
2011	2%	$8,347,378	1,118,894	404,558	95,805
2012	16%	$9,656,264	1,295,679	468,478	110,942
2013	32%	$12,759,468	1,710,296	618,390	146,443
Avg.	12%	12%	11%	13%	11%

I A N, L L C © 2014   1/2/14   TheInsidersGuides.com   10

Ibbotson Associates **Stocks average 11.4% per year, bonds 5%, CDs 3%.** Stocks have gone up as much as 54% and as low as –43% in 1 year, up to 28% or down to –12% in 5 years, up 20% or down 0% in 10 years, up 18% or up 3% in 20 years. Short term bonds have gone up 14% or up 0% in 1 year, up 11% or up 0% in 5 years, up 9% or up 0% in 10 years, up 10% or up 1% in 20 years.

Build your **Wealth Reserve**™ with savings from the Insider's Guides:

o Vehicle Insurance . . save up to $6,000 over 10 years
o Homeowner's Insurance . . . $2,000 over 10 years
o Life Insurance . . . $20,000 over 20 years
o Lawsuit Insurance . . . $3,000 over 10 years
o What NOT to buy: 101 products to avoid
o Health Insurance . . . $5,000 over 10 years
o Disability Insurance . . . $5,000 over 10 years
o Long Term Care . . . $40,000 over 20 years
o Education Funding . . . $20,000 over 18 years
o Retirement Spending . . . $1,000s over 30 years
o Banking . . . $3,000 each year
o Annuities . . . $20,000 in 20 years
o Mutual Funds/Securities . . . $3,000 each year
o Spending Plan: Reach every goal
o Self-Funded 'Bank' . . . $250,000 in 15 years
o Vehicle Purchase . . . $10,000 per vehicle
o Mortgage Purchase . . . $3,000 per contract
o **Wealth Reserve**™ . . . $1,000,000 in 25 years
o Wealth Transfer . . . $20,000 in 10 years
o Living Insurance . . . $120,000 over 20 years
o Self-insurance . . . $20,000 over 20 years
o Business Insurance: Buy only what you need
o Financial Independence for Women
o Survivors: Create Your Future Life

www.TheInsidersGuides.com

3

'Snoring' is the best way to create wealth!

People who are successful have **patience**.

This may seem a simple matter but many people who are not wealthy do not understand that you have to be patient in order to cultivate the assets that "grow by themselves." The independently wealthy buy assets that grow; not "things" that require them to pay out income for the rest of their lives. Master investor Warren Buffett said:

> We continue to make more money when snoring than when active.
> Berkshirehathaway.com

Time rewards you if you are patient. If every parent put just $2,000 in a low-cost stock market index fund at birth, every child might have between $1.2 and $4.7 million by age 65. Parents would not have to do a thing! Depending on the type of fund and account they used, $2,000 could compound at 10% to 12% per year—the historical average. Of course, in 65 years the buying power of $4 million would be about $1 million. Use this calculator to check how investments grows:
moneychimp.com/calculator/compound_interest_calculator.htm

Independents realize that it takes TIME to accumulate wealth. Hollywood exploits our childish fantasy of the instant millionaire. Real "working millionaires" don't get rich overnight. The most common method of making money is use the power of compounding. Independents have memorized the following chart so they know how their dreams will be fulfilled.

The miracle of compounding

Monthly	Accumulation at 12% per year									
	5	10	15	20	25	30	35	40	45	50
$100	$8,167	$23,004	$49,958	$98,925	$187,884	$349,496	$643,095	$1,176,477	$2,145,469	$3,905,834
$200	$16,334	$46,008	$99,916	$197,850	$375,768	$698,992	$1,286,190	$2,352,954	$4,290,938	$7,811,668
$300	$24,501	$69,012	$149,874	$296,775	$563,652	$1,048,488	$1,929,285	$3,529,431	$6,436,408	$11,717,502
$500	$40,835	$115,020	$249,790	$494,625	$939,420	$1,747,480	$3,215,475	$5,882,385	$10,727,346	$19,529,169

Invest $500 a month in a low-cost stock index fund and accumulate about $1,000,000 in 25 years. Use a tax-favored account like a Roth IRA, and you will pay zero taxes when the money is used. That could mean an extra 25% buying power. What plan could be easier to follow? The only ingredient needed is TIME. This is the essence of **The Simple Financial Life**.

The secret that independents have learned is patience. The vast majority of people with wealth live below their incomes so they can invest some of what they receive. The wealthy spend less than they earn—that's how they stay wealthy. They can't use the miracle of compounding if they spend their money.

Each $100 invested is worth $10,000 to you in the future

The patient independent person can buy whatever they want because they have planned for the expense. If you wanted to buy a house in 5 years, you could have the down payment of $40,000 by investing $500 a month. If $250 a month is what you can afford now, then it may take 9 years to get that house. Fine, but you could get your house. A bank CD will take you 12 years.

Almost every family wants to own their own home. Independents would be more likely to have the 20% down payment for a new home than others. They save the cost of the PMI insurance required by the lender to cover the lender's risk. Independents are likely to have higher deductibles on all their other insurance so that they benefit from years of saving $500 to $1000 on their premiums by self-insuring part of their risks.

Independents are savvy about saving for major purchases. They are more likely to shop around after doing their homework than to buy because they happen to wander through a store. They are more likely to use balanced and bond mutual funds than a traditional saving account or certificate of deposit. Depending on the amount needed and date of purchase, independents are comfortable using securities to accumulate the cash they need for major purchases. On average, a balanced mutual fund may earn 6-8% per year with more consistency than a stock mutual fund. You can experiment with the amounts and times needed to save for a purchase at moneychimp.com/calculator/compound_interest_calculator.htm. Enter $2000 per year, 30 years, 10 or 12 interest credited 12 times a year and compare what your nest egg could be worth. Enter $6000 ($500 x 12) per year, 10 years, 6% compounded 12 times and compare the result for college or down payment needs.

Finally, independents try to keep their financial lives simple by using only one mutual fund family. Some use only three mutual funds for all their needs. Some use 10. Since you are building this account for long-term accumulation, you should invest in all kinds of companies, around the world. Don't speculate on the hot ones.

You only need to buy THREE funds

Since independents believe that the cost of investing matters, they buy and hold low-cost stock mutual funds. They make regular and automatic additions to their accumulations. For long-term needs, stock ownership in US and non-US firms provides the best chance of success in accomplishing your goals.

The most efficient way to own companies for long term growth is to buy and hold stock mutual funds that represent the whole world market using "dollar cost averaging" of $100-$500 a month. Over periods greater than 10 years, studies show your returns will exceed those of 86% of investors. An equity index mutual fund with low fees can meet the requirements for long term wealth--$500 a month may reach a million dollars in 25 years if left to compound tax-FREE, using a Roth IRA.

> A **WEALTH RESERVE** may have only three funds

Few mutual fund families offer high quality services to the consistent investor at low cost. The independent investor need look no further than Vanguard or TIAA for a wide selection of equity funds. They provide exposure to full participation in every sector, and size and style that capitalism has to offer. No one company, sector or poor manager will deplete your accumulation over the long term if you use these firms. Your assets are growing by themselves at the lowest costs.

One fund family lets the new investor start small. Using a Roth IRA account, you can begin with $100 a month at TIAA. Both fund families earn high marks from financial rating agencies. In fact, Morningstar said, "The firm [TIAA] is widely known among the institutional crowd, and has a reputation for providing good, low-cost, risk-controlled funds, which this one definitely is. At 0.30%, 'its annual price tag is rivaled only by a scant few competitors', which helps burnish its very investor-friendly profile."

Both firms mentioned above provide long-term performance because less of your money goes to managers, brokers and marketing. The equity funds provide the returns of the market—10% to 12% over any period of over 10 years. There is no guarantee for the future but the probability is very high that stock funds will continue to provide the best hedge against inflation you can buy. Bond funds offer a less volatile return of 6-8% on average. Our strategy takes one hour to execute with either firm. Vanguard offers the Total Stock Market Index, Total International Stock Market Index, and the Total Bond Market Index for simplicity and diversified investing.

This makes for a Simple, Easy and Wise Plan.

Begin TODAY!

Remember the experience of Fred and Susan above. The insurance company executive said that the Reserve they have built up is the real meaning of insurance: it is **lifestyle protection**. He said that today it is even easier to create a **Wealth Reserve**™ because the Roth IRA allows most working people to use market securities for their important needs without paying any federal tax on the earnings—ever. Pension plans delay tax until retirement. You will pay NO tax unless you take the EARNINGS out early.

The **Wealth Reserve**™ Roth IRA lets you pay for a home and disabilities without penalty. You would be able to supplement a smaller Social Security check without any federal income taxes—Zero, Nothing, FREE.

Even if you did not start early, a **Wealth Reserve**™ can be created and used by most people because we are all living longer. The chart on page 39 shows how $166 per month, $2,000 a year has grown since 1950. Even late starters can create a **Wealth Reserve**™ of $249,000 to insure their lifestyle. The table below shows how patience paid off over the years for one client who invested $250 a month in an S&P 500 index account.

Client Tom's account, investing $3,000 per year, 1962-2003

Return	Balance
24%	3,720
16%	7,795
12%	12,091
-10%	13,582
24%	20,561
11%	26,153
-8%	26,821
4%	31,013
14%	38,775
19%	49,713
-14%	45,333
-26%	35,766
37%	53,110
24%	69,576
-8%	66,770
6%	73,956
18%	90,809
32%	123,827
-5%	120,486
22%	150,653
21%	185,920
6%	200,255
32%	268,297
19%	322,843
5%	342,135
17%	403,808
32%	536,987
-3%	523,787
31%	690,091
8%	748,538
10%	826,692
2%	846,286
38%	1,172,015
23%	1,445,268
33%	1,926,197
28%	2,469,372
21%	2,991,570
-9%	2,725,059
-12%	2,403,420
-22%	1,874,601
29%	2,412,905

The Roth IRA Rules

Contributions:

$5,500 ($6,500 over age 50) each year
Income under $132,000 (2016) single
married $194,000 (2016)

Distributions:

Tax-FREE for contributions.
And Tax-FREE for earnings if
Over age 59 1/2,
Account open 5 years,
Taxable earnings unless
Disabled,
First home ($10,000),
Death

Bonus:

Account can grow tax-FREE for life
Minimum distribution rules don't apply
Heirs don't pay income tax
Account has no maximum

Check with your tax preparer
https://www.irs.gov/publications/p590a/

4

Self-insure with your **Wealth Reserve**™

There is no better protection than having assets

This doesn't mean buying a lot of insurance. It means understanding the role of risk and reward in everyday decision-making. For instance, why pay for medical insurance in your car insurance policy when you already have medical insurance? Independents self-insure the risks they can afford to take.

Self-insurance means retaining part of the premiums and risk of any insurance contract. Many businesses self-insure in order to save money and control the risks of running a business. Many businesses self-insure their group life, unemployment compensation and health insurance. They avoid regulation. They pay a TPA to collect premiums and pay claims from a company account, sometimes in a tax haven. The company earns interest on the money they would have paid as premiums to an insurance company. The business buys a special policy to cover only the huge expenses like heart surgery.

An individual can gain the same advantages by buying high-deductible policies for car, home, health, disability, long-term care, and other insurance. Another form of self-insurance is to reduce the amount of term life insurance over time. This is the concept behind a **Wealth Reserve**™. Instead of paying $375 a month for $500,000 permanent life, a term policy costs $15 a month. You build your $1 million **Wealth Reserve**™ with the $360 balance. When the term becomes expensive by age 50, you can cut the coverage in half and use your own assets to self-insure the rest. By age 65, your kids are grown and your assets provide an income. NO life insurance is needed.

Your **Wealth Reserve**™ will cover your car and home deductibles as well as your supplemental health and long-term care risks. You can actually **drop some of your insurance**. Your **Wealth Reserve**™ protects you against many losses that are small and infrequent. The purpose of insurance is to transfer the risk of catastrophic loss to an entity that pools small premiums from many people to cover one big loss. Many people make the mistake of buying insurance for every single eventuality. Besides complicating your life, this is a waste of money.

Your life insurance policy must insure your life so that your family has an income to survive the transition to a different lifestyle, if you are not around. They need a sufficient amount to generate an income to replace yours. A $500,000 policy could provide $45,000 a year. They may want to pay off all or most of your bills. One term policy costing under $1 a day is sufficient to do this. You don't need insurance on your mortgage, car loan, credit cards, or home improvement loan. See Chapter 8.

Your **Wealth Reserve**™ **replaces permanent life insurance** as your security for the future. Almost every adult can purchase insurance *when* they need it. Contrary to industry hype, cash value life insurance is a terrible investment for a young person. (One viewer of this video said, "I am honestly purchasing whole life insurance from WM solely due to the music in this commercial."? youtube.com/watch?v=rj6uKxbOy_A&feature=related)

Create your **Wealth Reserve**™

Save $3,000 a year on financial products you need.
Create a $1 million **Wealth Reserve**™ with the savings.
Drop financial products you don't need—you're self-insured. Self-insure with your $1 million **Wealth Reserve**™.

Your **Wealth Reserve**™ consists of all the assets you own that "grow by themselves." A **Wealth Reserve**™ allows you to insure and finance yourself instead of giving your hard won income to your agent, banker or broker. Your **Wealth Reserve**™ allows you to provide for your own permanent life insurance, long-term care insurance, and disability insurance coverage.

> A **WEALTH RESERVE** provides lifestyle protection

Your **Wealth Reserve**™ provides cash for retirement funding. It can even pay for luxury cars, vacation homes and your own business start-up at a discount. Your **Wealth Reserve**™ allows you to buy liability (car and home) insurance at 30% less.

Your **Wealth Reserve**™ allows you to be financially independent like many of our members. It is TIME not investment skill that creates wealth. To repeat Mr Buffett statement about buy and hold stock mutual funds: berkshirehathaway.com

"We continue to make more money when snoring than when active."

How assets build your **Wealth Reserve**™

Monthly	Accumulation at 12% per year									
	5	10	15	20	25	30	35	40	45	50
$100	$8,167	$23,004	$49,958	$98,925	$187,884	$349,496	$643,095	$1,176,477	$2,145,469	$3,905,834
$200	$16,334	$46,008	$99,916	$197,850	$375,768	$698,992	$1,286,190	$2,352,954	$4,290,938	$7,811,668
$300	$24,501	$69,012	$149,874	$296,775	$563,652	$1,048,488	$1,929,285	$3,529,431	$6,436,408	$11,717,502
$500	$40,835	$115,260	$249,790	$494,625	$939,420	$1,747,480	$3,215,475	$5,882,385	$10,727,346	$19,529,169

Financially savvy people buy only the products and services they really need. We show you how they do it in each of the Insider's Guides: banking, mortgage, mutual funds, securities, annuity, life insurance, health insurance, long term care insurance, vehicle insurance, home insurance, lawsuit insurance, vehicle purchases . . . almost any product or service.

You can save up to $3,000 per year using The Insider's Guides. Smart independents don't spend that extra $3,000. They buy "assets that grow by themselves." They put their money into their own business or the stocks of public companies. That $3,000 becomes $3,202, then $6,811, then $10,877, until they have about $1,000,000 in 33 years, $2 mil in 40. This is your **Wealth Reserve**™.

Financially independent people have fun with their money. They enjoy buying assets that grow without the need to work more hours. They stop wasting their paychecks by making sure that the $3,000 they saved goes automatically into their business or the securities they own. They enjoy it so much that they find a way to save another $3,000 or $250 a month. If these independents work for someone else, they enroll in their employer's retirement plan when they receive a matching amount for their plan FREE. They start a tax-FREE Roth 401k or Roth IRA.

Where does that extra $250 a month come from? It comes from buying the financial products you really need, directly from quality providers like our insiders do. (theinsidersguides.com/about_us) By buying only what you need directly, without the middleperson, you can identify that $250 a month or more immediately. See the

EasySheet, below.

One member recently moved their mutual funds from Fidelity to Vanguard and saved over $3,000 a year. They were paying about $4,188 or 1.2% of their account values of $349,000 *each year*. Now they pay less than 0.20% or $698 per year. Their retirement funds will be $545,000 greater because they pay 0.2% instead of 1.2% every year until retirement. Compare your present fund to a low-cost leader to see the difference:
https://personal.vanguard.com/us/funds/tools.

What is a **Wealth Reserve**™?

Your **Wealth Reserve**™ consists of all the assets you own that "grow by themselves." That means your retirement plan at work. It means your rental real estate, your securities and mutual funds. It means your IRAs. It means your business, if you own one. It means your Keogh, SEP, and SIMPLE are your **Wealth Reserve**™ too. Most of your private property--vehicles, appliances, furniture, etc--are **NOT** your **Wealth Reserve**™. They wear out. They don't grow in value. They are expenses from your **Wealth Reserve**™.

Your **Wealth Reserve**™ may consist of many types of assets. In fact financially independent people never put "all their eggs in one basket." Even when they run a business full-time, they typically have only 25% of their wealth in the business. They spread it around—tax-favored retirement plans, rental real estate, and negotiable securities.

Financially independent people are independent because they use their income to buy more assets that "grow by themselves," NOT more things. Typically their **Wealth Reserve**™ allows them to feel comfortable because they

spend less than they make. If their income were to be cut for five or more years, they would be able to survive—keeping their family and home intact. They don't borrow money except to buy assets that earn more than the cost of the loan. Usually a mortgage or business loan is all they owe.

Most of our members use their **Wealth Reserve**™ for the bulk of their retirement plan. Some started early in their working life and consistently increased the proportion of their income designated for investments. By maximizing their 401k retirement plan contributions, they have reduced their taxable income. They pay less income tax now. Some obtain FREE contribution matches from their employer. Their **Wealth Reserve**™ growth is supercharged. However, they pay taxes on retirement money.

Their assets grow because of the extra contributions and because their earnings are not taxed now. The contributions reduce their taxable income each year. Also most of their assets are invested in low-cost mutual funds. They decided which mutual funds to use inside their retirement plans based upon the fact that 86% of fund managers cannot beat the market averages even though they charge over 1.2% extra to try every year. Members favor low-cost index funds. *BusinessWeek* Apr 2009.

Most of our members also own other mutual funds, securities and real estate in various taxable, tax-deferred and tax-FREE accounts. Some have left employers with retirement plans after years of accumulation. Most of them have opened rollover IRA accounts and had the new trustee move the money so they continue compounding without spending it and paying tax. Tax-deferred compounding was all that was available until recently.

Many members now have three or more mutual funds with one company. Some members have seen their **Wealth Reserve**™s grow dramatically over the years even though they don't buy the most publicized funds. Some members invest 10% of their income, some more and some less. Most members with sizable accounts started investing about 5% and increased the percentage as their goals became clear. They saved for their first home down payment, college funds, vacations and cars. Members continue to increase the amount invested by using The Insider's Guides to cut the commissions and fees on their financial service needs.

How your **Wealth Reserve**™ saves you up to 40%

Financially savvy members have used our Insider's Guide to Vehicle Insurance to help them save up to $6,000 over 10 years.

We explain that standard vehicle policies charge for coverage that duplicates existing coverage for most people. We explain what you need and don't need and why to keep the deductible high. We show you where to buy if you have a problem in your record, or you have vehicles "at high risk." If you are a safe experienced driver, you can benefit by switching to certain insurers. One of them has been rated No. 1 in customer satisfaction for 4 consecutive years by JD Power and pays YOU dividends. It has the highest A++ ratings. Why pay extra commission and subsidize other people's poor driving habits?

Not every member can qualify for all 13 categories of savings we list. However, our Insider provides enough "tricks of the trade" to help almost every member save hundreds of dollars. For example, a member in Hewlett, NY switched and saved over $1,500 on his three vehicles. Instead of spending that $1,500, he has $125 deducted from his checking account monthly by a low-cost mutual fund trustee. He is using a Roth IRA to shield his earnings from any taxation. His goal is to have an extra $125,000 tax-FREE when he retires to cover his long-term care needs, if any.

John K. of New Jersey spent 20 minutes with his new carrier's call center agent. His premium fell 33% from $2,029.30 to $1,358 for 2 Toyotas with full coverage. The carrier is rated A++ by A.M.Best. Claims service is open 24 hours and it has the same complaint rate as State Farm in New Jersey. A year ago, he saved $567 by switching from another carrier.

This member picked the mutual fund inside his Roth IRA specifically so that his assets grew at a different rate than the other ones he owns in his retirement fund at work. His current **Wealth Reserve**™ is sufficient to "loan" him the money for the $1,000 deductible on his new vehicle insurance policy, should he need it this year. By next year, the $125 a month savings will cover the possible deductible while he earns the capital gains that his insurer used to keep each year. Also his **Wealth Reserve**™ will be growing with an additional $125 per month that he was wasting on the insurance before.

A member from Montclair, NJ used our <u>Insider's Guide to Homeowners Insurance</u> to save $5,000 over 10 years. Again, you probably don't need some of the coverage that is hidden in your existing policy. Our Insider explains what you need and don't need, why to keep the deductible high, and when **NOT to call your agent or insurer.** He shows you where to buy if you have a home "at high risk." If you have never had a claim, you may benefit by switching to a "direct writer." Why subsidize others' claims? In some states, you can save 100% or more by using our Insiders' hints.

Another member in Vermont dropped his life insurance after realizing that his adult children did not need the protection any more. Further, after consulting our <u>Insider's Guide to Retirement Plans</u> he determined to invest aggressively to insure that he would have enough to retire when he wanted to. He used our <u>Insider's Guide to Buying Mutual Funds and Securities</u> to save 1% a year on his choice of mutual funds and brokerage firms.

The $156 a month he was spending on life insurance is now buying assets that "grow by themselves." He is increasing his **Wealth Reserve**™ with money he did not need to spend on insurance. Instead of spending the $156 a month, he is investing it to self-insure his lifestyle. He plans to replace his current car in five years. He read our <u>Insider's Guide to Vehicle Purchases</u> and will save about $10,000 on a luxury sedan. Building your **Wealth Reserve**™ protects you against giving money away to banks, especially the $3,000 to $4,000 in interest most people pay every year on credit cards and car loans.

Making your money work for 10 years in your **Wealth Reserve**™ can provide about $51,000, enough for a home down payment, car, vacation, etc. You will have paid only $30,000 ($3,000 for 10 years) for that $51,000. You borrow from your "bank" to pay cash. See the past market returns on page 39.

You don't have to have extra money or time

The **Wealth Reserve**™ strategy works because you don't have to *find* new money or 2nd job to build your **Wealth Reserve**™. You use the money you already spend for financial services that you decide you don't need. Instead of buying a car or appliance and paying up to 5 times the price by financing it, you pay cash. However, the cash from your **Wealth Reserve**™ is special. It is 'compounded' cash (the $51,000 described above cost you only $30,000!). You pay less because you planned ahead. See our

Insider's Guide to Banking to avoid paying FIVE times the price for financed items.

WARNING: This book offers a strategy to self-insure and self-fund your financial needs. Our Insider's Guides show you how to drop services you may not need. However, before you change your current accounts, make certain that the alternative plan is in place. Do not close the old account/policy until you have tried the services from your new providers and started your Wealth Reserve™.

Typically, members are "buy-and-hold" investors. They do not try to time the market by buying the hot stock or fund. That activity only benefits the brokers and leaves the average investor earning 3.79% according to a DALBARinc.com study. Some members use Modern Portfolio Theory (riskglossary.com) to increase returns as they reduce risk.

Some members have chosen low-cost index funds to keep their **Wealth Reserve**™ building simple. These members believe that broad market indexes provide their best chance of accumulating at 10%-12% annually over the long haul. They don't consider themselves risk takers but are comfortable leaving 100% of their long-term money in stock funds. Their short-term goals are accomplished by funding low-cost balanced funds. They used Morningstar.com to screen for the funds they use.

Other members are very well informed about the companies in their business field or employment. They keep investing in these few firms over the long-term. They buy stocks with deep discount brokers. Some pay zero commissions. Members explain how they do it in our Insider's Guide to Buying Mutual Funds and Securities.

How your **Wealth Reserve**™ works

An example of how a **Wealth Reserve**™ works over a lifetime was provided above. Fred and Susan started creating a fund many years before our Network was formed. They started out just saving for their daughter's college expenses at birth. They kept using their 'college fund' for more than just college. They used it like a **Wealth Reserve**™ to self-insure and self-fund their lifetime needs.

This is a summary of the story of how Fred and Susan created and used their **Wealth Reserve**™.

Fred and Susan had a baby—Natalie—in 1975. They lived in lower Manhattan. They wanted to protect their new child's future and to have college money. They picked Dow stocks with the highest yield and the lowest price [dogsofthedow.com]. This was in 1975 or '76.

Dividends were reinvested and the income tax was not outrageous. They invested without a broker in plans called DSP and DRIPS (enrolldirect. now us.computershare.com/). They had $5,000 from gifts and they contributed $6 a day ($350 monthly). Most of the companies they picked allowed them to buy stocks without a broker's fee. By the time Natalie was 18, Fred and Susan had about $300,000.

They kept putting money in each month. During the bad years —you know 1977-78, they had second thoughts. But Susan kept them on track.

They had a car accident a few years after they started and needed money to pay for the policy deductible. They were saving about $200 a year by taking the $1,000 deductible. So they needed to sell $1,000 of stock. They sold stock that was down that year. In fact, I think they did not have to pay any tax on that sale. Anyway, that $1,000 sale did not hurt them. They still ended up with about $300,000. And remember, all this time—18 years—they have saved $200 on their car insurance. That's $3,600 of the $75,600 ($350 X 12 months X 18 years) they invested. That is $300,000 for $75,600 invested.

Like most families, they wanted a house. The cost of the down payment--$15,000—came from Natalie's college fund. They still ended up with about $300,000. But what they found was that some of the stocks had done worse than others. They sold the worst ones, paying little tax on the gain.

They purchased the house with the $15,000 and avoided the mortgage insurance that bankers usually charge those who have less than a 20% down payment. This saved them more money each year too.

In a sense then, part of the $350 they paid each month for the college fund was actually paid for by the savings from the fact they had enough of a down payment not to need private mortgage insurance. They saved on their homeowners by picking a $5,000 deductible and not needing expensive extras, like coverage for jewelry or furs. They saved on credit life, disability, unemployment, and PMI insurance that the mortgage bank tried to add on to their mortgage. All these helped pay for the college fund.

In order to protect the $300,000 fund and all their other assets, Fred found out about umbrella liability insurance. For $210 a year, Susan and Fred would have $1,000,000 coverage in case they were sued and needed to pay a lawyer to defend themselves. Even if the accident was their fault, the policy covered the judgment and the lawyer fees too.

They were finally ready for Natalie to go to college. Of course she didn't need the money all at once. And when she made her decision about where to go to college she chose a very good state college that cost only $10,000 a year.

During this time educational loans were very cheap. So Fred and Susan decided to let the college fund grow—20% to 25% a year—during the 90's. They knew this was unusual because the average gain for Dow stocks was 12% a year. They let the loans grow for the first two years until they could see that they had earned $60,000 for two years straight. We discussed this and decided this can't last. So they sold enough stock to pay the loans and the tax of 20% on the stock earnings. Now they realized they did not have to worry about the college loans any more.

They stopped paying for life insurance policies that she and Fred owned. This saved them another $2,500 a year and they continued to invest the $350 per month. It was getting easier with fewer expenses. As a backup emergency fund, they took out a home equity line of credit that cost them nothing—no fees or closing costs. They pay the market rate only *if* they need to use the line for emergencies.

Susan was disabled within the year. She no longer had disability insurance from work. She was not able to work at all. They decided to cut back on their entertainment, vacation, and hobbies in order to get by on Fred's salary. They also had an emergency expense. They had to sell stock to pay $10,000 for Fred's parent's home repair. The tax on the earnings of the stocks did not push them into the next tax bracket, so they are actually paying much less tax this year anyway.

The next year after Natalie graduated; Susan and Fred decided to start their own business. Fred would work part-time. The college fund—now $600,000 or so—gave them the feeling that they would have incomes until they got the store into the black. The store liability policy was not too bad after Susan picked a higher deductible. Fred's job would provide the health insurance they needed.

The store business allows Fred and Susan to deduct many of the normal expenses associated with their activities. The 'college' fund, no longer for college, allows them to save more on the protection they need for retirement. They attended a seminar on long-term care insurance and decided that they can afford it but don't need it. According to page 6 of the Shopper's Guide they received at the seminar, the chance of Fred needing expensive care is 4%; Susan 13%. [See our <u>Insider's Guide to Long-term Care Insurance</u>.]

If they spent $4,000 a year for up to 30 years, they may never get to use that $120,000 [$2,000 each, times 30 years] because they both are in good health. Anyway, 25% of LTC buyers drop it within two years. So, Fred and Susan put the $4,000 in their tax-advantaged retirement plan, connected with their business. This will add another $600,000 for any emergency, including remodeling their home for easy access and hiring a home health aide. Worst case, they have assets and a business which helps them with health care.

Lifestyle Protection

A **Wealth Reserve**™ is usually started when people get motivated to save and invest, usually when they have a child. Every one of our members wishes they had started their **Wealth Reserve**™ or 'self-insurance fund' earlier than they did.

The Reserve Fred and Susan have built up is the real meaning of insurance: it is **lifestyle protection**. Today it is even easier to create a **Wealth Reserve**™ because the Roth IRA allows most working people to use market securities for their important needs without paying any federal tax on the earnings—*ever*. The Roth lets you pay for a 1st home and disabilities <u>without any federal income tax or penalty</u>. Contributions are always tax-FREE. Today, members would be able to supplement their pensions with the $900,000 or so they have accumulated without any federal income taxes—Zero, Nothing, <u>FREE</u>. <u>fairmark.com/rothira/disttop.htm</u>

If you expect to live another 10 years, a **Wealth Reserve**™ can be created and used by most people because we are all living longer. The chart on page 39 shows how $167 per month, $2,000 a year, has grown over a number of years. Even late starters can make a **Wealth Reserve**™ of $249,000 to self-insure their lifestyle now and in retirement.

If your **Wealth Reserve**™ is not depleted by extra health care costs in retirement and extra living expenses due to a longer life and higher living costs due to inflation, you have the satisfaction of knowing that your Reserve can pass to heirs on a "stepped-up basis." That means NO INCOME tax to heir. The annuity and regular IRA do not afford them this kindness. With an annuity and regular IRA, your heirs will get stuck with the income tax bill on the gains at their tax rate. Your **Wealth Reserve**™ can become the Reserve for their families.

Building your **Wealth Reserve**™ can be done by anyone: Invest as little as $100 a month AND cut out wasteful spending on financial products and services you don't need.

Below is the list of savings that our member, the King family, shared with us. They dropped some of the insurance coverage they didn't need—accident, towing and health on their auto insurance, jewels and furs on home insurance, mortgage insurance called PMI, permanent (whole) life. They raised the deductible for their auto and homeowners insurance. They switched mutual fund companies to save annual fees. They are paying off their credit cards and switching to cards with lower fees. They switched banks and cable/telephone contracts. They are adding $600 a month to their **Wealth Reserve**™. They will have enough for emergencies, accident deductibles and home repairs.

Most importantly, the King family will reach their goals: College funds, Vacation home, Small business start up, Travel, Luxury vehicles, Retirement, Foundation creation, and a Legacy.

Finally, a prudent independent has a legal will to protect their children and a power of attorney to protect themselves when they can't. These documents can be executed by you for under $60. nolo.com/index.cfm. The reason you need a will is simply that it makes it easier to gain custody of your child, assets and legacy left by your departed spouse. The reason you need a POA is simply that you need an advocate when you can't make decisions yourself. Usually your spouse will be your advocate. You need a living will for the same reason. The case of Terri Schiavo in 2005 made it clear to all why you don't want Congress deciding what you should have decided yourself. en.wikipedia.org/wiki/Government_involvement_in_the_Terri_Schiavo_case

You must start today. Create your **Wealth Reserve**™ following the steps above. Ruthlessly consider if you really need to pay for each financial product you now pay for. Use The Insiders Guides to decide. They were written by **unbiased advisors** who have nothing to gain from your decisions.

EasySheet   Where your **Wealth Reserve**™ contributions come from:

Monthly expense **savings** for the King family: Your family:

Vehicle insurance (2)	$ 56	$ _____
Homeowners insurance	$ 11	$ _____
Permanent life insurance	$ 167	$ _____
Mutual fund fees	$ 83	$ _____
Mortgage insurance PMI	$ 103	$ _____
Accident insurance at work	$ 33	$ _____
Umbrella liability insurance	$ -18 (bought new)	$ _____
Bank fees	$ 10	$ _____
Credit card finance charges	$ 125	$ _____
Other fees, charges	$ 30	$ _____

Total amount saved monthly $ 600 $ _____

    Saved annually   **$7,200** $ _____

Possible Wealth Reserve™ **for the King family**   Your family:

Ten year accumulation $139,403 $ _____
($7200 for 10 years at 12%)

Goals
    College funds   Vacation home

Twenty year accumulation $599,489 $ _____
($7200 for 20 years at 12%)

Goals
    Small business start-up   Travel
    Luxury vehicles

Thirty year accumulation $2,117,948 $ _____
($7200 for 30 years at 12%)

Goals
    Retirement
    Legacy   Foundation creation

Accumulation estimates assume an investment in a market index fund with the same world economic performance in the future as in the last 50 years. Use this calculator to find how much you can accumulate:
moneychimp.com/calculator/compound_interest_calculator.htm

5

Create your own Self-Funded 'Bank'
Pay up to 40% less for any item

When you fund your **Wealth Reserve**™, you are creating your Self-Funded 'bank.' It is the assets you have accumulated that "grow by themselves." The assets allow you to finance your lifestyle purchases instead of giving your hard won income to your credit card banker or lender. Your Self-Funded 'bank' allows you to provide cash for college, cars, vacations and your own business start-up–whatever.

Your Self-Funded 'bank' helps you become financially independent. The key to growing assets is TIME, not investment skill or fast trading. Financially savvy people buy only the products and services they really need. They can save thousands of dollars per year by

> **Saved 40%**
>
> Ms. Lee wanted to buy a duplex for rental income. She needed $60,000 down payment to avoid PMI. She invested $250 per month for 10 years in her 'bank.' She earned $27,456 on her $30,000 deposit. She bought a two family house for $300,000 and her tenant's rent pays for the mortgage and ½ the utilities. Ms. Lee is so thrilled, she saves $500 in her 'bank' so she can buy a bigger property.

using their 'bank' to loan themselves the money for insurance deductibles, cars, a down payment, and any expenses they would normally finance. Smart independents don't waste that extra money on interest and fees. Instead, they use their income to buy assets that "grow by themselves." They put their money in their own business, rental real estate and the stocks of public companies. The savings can become $1,000,000 in 40 years when invested. If you are smart, you will repay your 'bank' so that you have a Reserve for later expenses. You can use this calculator (moneychimp.com/calculator/compound_interest_calculator.htm) to estimate your accumulations for specific goal amounts.

Financially independent people *have fun* with their money. They enjoy buying assets that grow without the need to work more hours. They stop wasting their paychecks by making sure that their money is invested automatically in their 401k, their business, or **Wealth Reserve**™. They enjoy being financially free of money worries so much that they find a way to save another $3,000 a year. Eventually, they don't have to work for someone else—their money does all the work for them.

Where can you find the $250 a month?

You can learn which financial products you really need and buying them directly from quality providers. By buying only what you need, directly, without the middle person, you can identify that $250 a month and more.

For example, one member of our network moved their mutual funds from Fidelity to Vanguard and saved over $3,000 a year. They were paying about $4,188 or 1.2% of their current account values of $349,000 *each year* for the last 10 years. Now they pay less than 0.20% or $698 per year. Their retirement fund will be $545,000 larger because they pay **0.2% instead of 1.2%** per year until retirement. Broker-sold 'load' funds are **NOT** better. Compare your present funds to a low-cost leader to see the difference: https://personal.vanguard.com/us/funds/tools/costcompare.

How assets build your Self-Funded 'bank'
That crazy chart again!

Monthly Accumulation at 12% per year										
	5	10	15	20	25	30	35	40	45	50
$100	$8,167	$23,004	$49,958	$98,925	$187,884	$349,496	$643,095	$1,176,477	$2,145,469	$3,905,834
$200	$16,334	$46,008	$99,916	$197,850	$375,768	$698,992	$1,286,190	$2,352,954	$4,290,938	$7,811,668
$300	$24,501	$69,012	$149,874	$296,775	$563,652	$1,048,488	$1,929,285	$3,529,431	$6,436,408	$11,717,502
$500	$40,835	$115,020	$249,790	$494,625	$939,420	$1,747,480	$3,215,475	$5,882,385	$10,727,346	$19,529,169

What is a Self-Funded 'bank'?

Your Self-Funded 'bank' consists of the assets you accumulate from your contributions that "grow by themselves." Usually, these are the shares of mutual funds you buy every month. The Self-Funded 'bank' may consist of many types of assets. In fact, financially independent people never put "all their eggs in one basket." They buy different mutual funds holding growth and value stocks, real estate, and other negotiable securities.

Financially independent people are independent because they use their income to buy more assets that "grow by themselves," NOT more 'things.' Typically, their Self-Funded 'bank' allows them to feel comfortable because they spend less than they make. If their income were to be reduced for five or more years, they would be able to survive—keeping their family and home intact. They don't borrow money from traditional banks unless they can earn more than the cost of the loan. Usually a mortgage or business loan is all they use: Never car or personal loans.

Most of our clients use their Self-Funded 'bank' to supplement their retirement funds, later in life. Typically they started investing later in their working life. They consistently increased the proportion of their income designated for investments because they started late. By starting your fund early, you are maximizing your retirement plan. You are also reducing your taxable income since you use a Roth IRA. You will pay less income tax. If you understand how to invest, you may obtain FREE contribution matches from your employer in a Roth 401k. This will allow you to use your 'bank' to secure your lifestyle without debt.

Your Self-Funded 'bank' may grow tax-DEFERRED (401k) and tax-FREE, so growth is supercharged. Your assets grow because of steady contributions and because the earnings are not taxed NOW. Hopefully, most of your assets are invested in low-cost global stock mutual funds.

Over time, you will see your Self-Funded 'bank' grow dramatically during some years. Even though your mutual funds may not make the headlines, don't sell them and try to buy the ones in the news. Successful investing comes from buying every month so that when the share price is down, you receive more. No one can control the up and down of the markets but you can avoid high commissions and fees on the 'hot' mutual fund of the day. So, avoid buying the hot and then selling when they cool.

How a Self-Funded 'bank' saves up to 40%

Financially savvy client/members have used our Insider's Guide to Vehicle Purchase (in our *Guide to Buying Discount Financial Services*) to help them save $20,000 or more on a luxury vehicle purchase. For example, some years ago, Danielle bought a three year old Lexus ES 300 for $16,000 cash. She saved 30% by buying a quality used car. She paid cash.

Note: If she had obtained a 7.5% loan for 5 years, she would have paid $321 per month (Bankrate.com calculator). Total paid: $19,260 for a $16,000 car. She paid cash from her Self-Funded 'bank.' She used the $321 a month to

> **Save 30% or more**
> Danielle of New Jersey spent 40 minutes online to find 3 luxury car candidates within 50 miles of her home. She faxed each seller a bid of $1,000 under the asking price. She got two affirmatives. She found a three-year old Lexus for $16,000. She brought cash within 24 hours of the fax. The dealer's service record was complete.

make money during those 5 years. Danielle, who set up her 'bank' years ago, earned $26,500 in those 5 years. She did not pay the interest ($3,260) on the loan AND she is ahead by $29,760 less $16,000 or $13,760. This is why the independently wealthy buy luxury used cars for cash from their 'bank.' They keep building the 'bank' with contributions invested by the trustee automatically.

Another member in California dropped his life insurance after realizing that his adult children did not need the protection any more. Further, after consulting our Insider's Guide to Retirement Plans he determined to invest aggressively to insure that he would have enough to retire when he wanted to. He used our Insider's Guide to Buying Mutual Funds and Securities to save 1% a year on his choice of mutual funds and brokerage firms. *The Insiders' Guides to Buying Discount Financial Services: Buy Direct and Save $3,000 Every Year* at theinsidersguides.com/.

The $176 a month he was spending on whole life insurance is now buying assets that "grow by themselves." He is increasing his Self-Funded 'bank' with money he did not need to spend on insurance. Instead of spending the $176 a month on a new car, he is investing it. He plans to replace his current model in five years.

He read our Insider's Guide to Vehicle Purchases and will save using the tips of our insider—a real car dealer.

Building your Self-Funded 'bank' protects you against giving money away to banks, especially the $250-$350 in interest most people pay every month on credit cards and car loans. For example, many people will have to pay $161 per month for 10+ years to pay off the average debt of $10,050 at 15%. They will spend at least $19,360 to pay off that $10,050. (If their rate is 25%, they will pay $25,080 for $10,050.) They pay almost *double* for that same $10,050! bankrate.com

But that's not all—THE **REAL COST** IS MORE!

Think of it. If they did not have to use that $161 each month to pay off the $10,050 and $9,310 in interest, they would be able to use the $161 per month to make money. They could have made about *$37,036* in the 10 years using a mutual fund. So the REAL cost of that $10,050 debt is actually $56,396!! The lender gets the $19,360 (to pay the debt over time) and **they gave up** earning $37,036 from the $161 payment per month for 10 years. They gave up the down payment on a house!

That $10,050 in debt costs most people about $56,396!!!
FIVE TIMES MORE

Making $250 per month *work* for 10 years in their Self-Funded 'bank' can provide about $51,000, enough for a home down payment, car, vacation, etc. You will have contributed $30,000 ($3,000 for 10 years) for that $51,000. You can borrow from your 'bank' to pay cash for anything. It is special cash. Your **'bank' cash is worth 40% more than you paid for it over time.**

You don't have to give up a *latte*

If you pay your Self-Funded 'bank' back, you can buy more things you need at "40% off." This strategy works because you don't have to *find* new money to build your Self-Funded 'bank.' You use the money you save from DISCOUNT financial services. Instead of buying a car or appliance on credit and paying up to 5 times the price by financing it, you pay cash. See our Insider's Guide to Banking to avoid paying other bank charges.

Typically, our members are "buy-and-hold" investors. They do not try to time the market by buying the hot stock or fund. That activity only benefits the brokers and leaves the average investor earning **3.79%** according to a DALBARinc.com study. Some members use Modern Portfolio Theory (riskglossary.com) to increase returns as they reduce risk.

> WARNING: This Guide offers a strategy to self-fund their financial needs. Our Insider's Guides show them how to drop services they may not need. However, before they change their current accounts, make certain that the alternative plan is in place. Do not close the old account until they have tried the services from their new providers.

Some members have chosen low-cost index funds to keep their Self-Funded 'bank'-building simple. These members believe that broad market indexes provide their best chance of accumulating at 12% annually over the long haul. They don't consider themselves risk takers. They are comfortable leaving 100% of their long-term money in stock mutual funds. Their short-term goals are accomplished by funding low-cost balanced or bond funds.

Other members are very well informed about the companies in their businesses or employment. They keep investing in these few firms over the long-term. They buy stocks with deep discount brokers. Some pay $0 commissions. Members explain how they do it in our Insider's Guide to Buying Mutual Funds and Securities. Check how they do it.

How your Self-Funded 'bank' works

An example of how your Self-Funded 'bank' works over a lifetime was provided in a previous chapter. Fred and Susan started creating a fund many years before they needed it. They started out just saving for their daughter's college expenses at birth. They kept using their college fund for more than just college. They used it to 'self-fund' their lifetime needs. To review how Fred and Susan used their 'college' fund as a Self-Funded 'bank':

1. Fred and Susan had a baby—Natalie—in 1975. They wanted to protect their new child's future and to have college money.
2. They agreed on buying stocks because they could hold them without paying tax on the increased value until they needed the money.
3. They wanted a house. The cost of the down payment—$15,000—came from Natalie's college fund. They still ended up with about $300,000. They found that most of the $15,000 withdrawal was money they had already paid tax on.

> **THEIR "COLLEGE" FUND BECAME A SELF-FUNDED 'BANK'**

4. They were finally ready for Natalie to go to college. They had $300,000 available for her when she was 18 years old. She made her decision about where to go to college she chose a very good college that cost only $10,000 a year.
5. During this time, educational loans were very cheap. Accordingly, Fred and Susan decided to let the college fund grow —20% to 25% a year—during the 90's. They knew this was unusual because the average gain for Dow stocks was 12% a year. They let the loans grow for the first two years until they could see that they had earned $60,000 for two years straight. They sold enough stock to pay the loans and the tax of 20% on the stock earnings. At this time, they realized they did not have to worry about the college loans any more.
6. As a backup emergency fund, they took out a home equity line of credit that cost them nothing—no fees or closing costs. They pay the market rate only *if* they need to use the line for emergencies.
7. They had to sell stock to pay $10,000 for Fred's parent's home repair. The tax on the earnings of the stocks did not push them into the next tax bracket, so they are actually paying much less tax this year anyway.
8. Susan and Fred decided to start their own business. Fred would work part-time. Susan would work full-time in what she loved—framing people's pictures.
9. The store business allows Fred and Susan to deduct many of the normal expenses associated with their activities. It also allows them to create another pension where they can contribute up to $49,000 (2010).

Lifestyle Protection

A Self-Funded 'bank' is usually started when people get motivated to save and invest, usually when they plan a family or house purchase. Every one of our members wishes they had started their Self-Funded 'bank' earlier than they did. You can make that dream come true for your life by starting your 'bank' now.

Some have started a self-funded 'bank' for their kids. By putting $2,000 in individual stocks or a stock mutual fund for 8 years before age 25, the child could have almost $40,000 by age 30, $100,000 by age 40, $250,000 by age 50, and $1,000,000 by age 65. This does not interfere with the child's or grandchild's own financial aid or retirement savings plan at work. A Roth IRA makes the money tax-FREE.

This self-funded 'bank' provides money for purchasing anything without paying up to 5 times the price in interest and lost earnings. As we have seen, it is easy to create a Self-Funded 'bank' because the Roth IRA allows most working people to use market securities for their important needs without paying any federal tax on the earnings—*ever*. The Roth lets them pay for a 1st home and disabilities without any federal income tax or penalty. Taking their contributions is FREE. If they paid their 'bank' back, they would be able to rebuild the $1,000,000 for tax-FREE retirement income. Also, each year they paid no federal income taxes—Zero, Nothing. fairmark.com/rothira/disttop.htm

A Self-Funded 'bank' can be created even if you did not start early. Late starters can make a Self-Funded 'bank' of $249,790 in about 15 years. Late starters can find the $500 a month contributions just like the King family did—cutting duplicate products and overcharges on their current financial services using our Guides.

If they have repaid their Self-Funded 'bank' in time, it will provide an income in retirement. You can even provide a Self-Funded 'bank' to your heirs tax-FREE as a Roth IRA beneficiary. An annuity or regular IRA does not afford them this kindness. Your heirs will get stuck with the income tax bill on the gains at their tax rate, too.

Start your Self-Funded 'bank' today. Using this strategy, you can be 'bank' President in 30 minutes. Later, when you have determined that your retirement income is adequate, your Self-Funded 'bank' can become the basis for your own nonprofit § 501(c)(3) family foundation. http://www.foundationsource.com/

Warren Buffett, best investor of our time, gives advice:
'My wealth has come from a combination of living in America, some lucky genes, and **compound interest**.'

'Whether we're talking about socks or stocks, I like buying quality merchandise when it is marked down.'

'Investors should remember that excitement and expenses are their enemies. And if they insist on trying to time their participation in equities, they should try to be fearful when others are greedy and greedy when others are fearful.'

'The stock market serves as a relocation center at which money is moved from the active to the patient.'

'Investors making purchases in an overheated market need to recognize that it may often take an extended period for the value of even an outstanding company to catch up with the price they paid.'

'The most common cause of low prices is pessimism — sometimes pervasive, sometimes specific to a company or industry. We want to do business in such an environment, not because we like pessimism but because we like the prices it produces. It's optimism that is the enemy of the rational buyer.'

'I try to buy stock in businesses that are so wonderful that an idiot can run them. Because sooner or later, one will.'

'Success in investing doesn't correlate with I.Q. once you're above the level of 125. Once you have ordinary intelligence, what you need is the temperament to control the urges that get other people into trouble in investing.'

'We've long felt that the only value of stock forecasters is to make fortune tellers look good. Even now, I continue to believe that short-term market forecasts are poison and should be kept locked up in a safe place, away from children and also from grown-ups who behave in the market like children.'

'Our favorite holding period is forever.'

It is the amount we KEEP that matters!

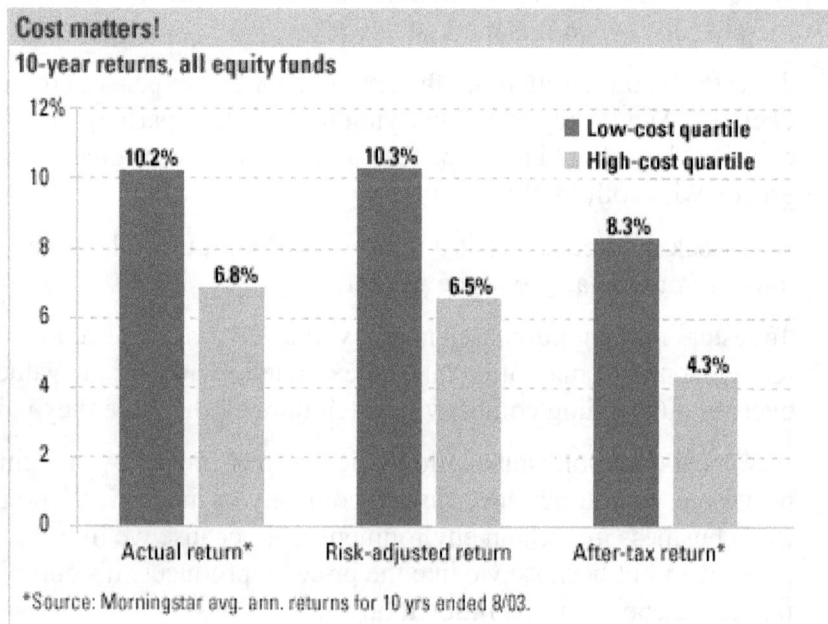

6

The Insider's Guide to Disability Insurance: Cash is a better plan

Do you need it?   Only if,

? Your employer does not provide it, or
? You are self-employed or own a small business.

Save $12,000 over 10 years

How will you pay your bills if you can't work?

According to a survey by the LIFE Foundation, 70 percent of working American adults say they could only afford to take off for one month or less of unpaid vacation before everyday expenses would force them to return to work.

You may <u>not need disability insurance if you have a financial plan to deal with temporary partial disability</u>, the most likely event. Many people are already covered at work if the injury takes place on the job (workers' compensation). Your employer may also pay for group coverage: sick days plus short-term disability pay. Your plan may rely on the fact that your spouse has an income. Finally, your plan may rely on a "self-insurance" **Wealth Reserve**™. This is the best 'insurance' since money can be used for other needs too.

> Mr S. age 40, office worker, found income protection from Unum, the largest insurer. Two years of $2300 monthly benefits after waiting 90 days from illness or accident costs $81 per month. Mr S receives a year of salary for catastrophic. Rate is guaranteed and can't be canceled.

If your family can survive on one salary for a few months, you could save money on a long-term disability policy. Since <u>most people will never need to use a disability insurance (DI) policy</u>, you save the cost of premiums. There are no refunds.

Most DI contracts have a deductible: a waiting or "elimination" period—90 or 180 days—before you can even file a claim. Thus, you need to have 3 to 6 months of expenses in an emergency fund anyway. Once you file a claim, you may receive only 50% of your salary for 1 or 2 years. This still may require the use of your own emergency fund. Most contracts expect you to return to *some* work as soon as possible in order to aid recovery.

Full long-term disability is very rare. If you are in good health and not accident prone, you might make insurance premium payments for a long time and <u>never see a dime</u>. Paying the premium to your own **Wealth Reserve**™ makes more sense since you can then use the funds for other financial needs. A **Wealth Reserve**™ grows tax-FREE, compounding your earnings over time, so when you need it, you receive more than you contributed. You keep the earnings on your premiums instead of the insurance company.

If your family has only one source of income, you coverage can be affordable if your occupation is not dangerous or exotic. DI is usually for a short period, in order to make a transition to another situation. It is not a windfall. Many large employers offer it in a group plan in coordination with other benefits like sick leave. Most often, individual DI is purchased by professionals and business owners. The <u>cost is born by their business</u>.

In the decision if DI is right for you, consider your health history, occupation risk, other family resources, and income. A sole earner in business for themselves cannot leave their family in the lurch if they are a highly compensated surgeon. On the other hand, an office worker with a working spouse may not need coverage. Disability is usually temporary. Only a tiny percentage of workers are disabled for life. DI is a very <u>expensive emergency fund</u>. Despite Aflac's duck TV spots, most of us don't need DI just cash which you will have more of *without* a policy.

Both of these individuals can use a self-insurance plan. Both need to build a **Wealth Reserve**™ for this financial risk as well as all the others. An individual disability plan can consist of a combination of spousal earnings supplemented by the **Wealth Reserve**™. This provides the security the family needs and saves a lot of wasted premium. Instead of paying an insurer, you buy assets that grow by themselves to save for yourself.

For instance, you can invest $100 a month for 10 years and have a benefit of $23,000 if you need it. This will carry most middle-income families for the most common short-term disability needs. This same principle can work for the surgeon but at a higher amount. $500 a month for 10 years can produce over a $100,000.

If these contributions are made to a tax-advantaged account like a **Wealth Reserve**™ there is NO penalty: exception for disability income if the earnings are needed. There is no penalty when you use your Roth IRA for income when a doctor has determined that your disability will be of "long, continued and indefinite duration." irs.gov/publications/p590/ch01.html#en_US_2011_publink1000230896

Unlike the DI policy, you don't give away the $12,000 or $60,000 you paid for your self-insurance protection. You are creating a reserve for other financial needs and wealth for your retirement and legacy. After 20 or 30 years of contributions, you have a long-term care plan and retirement supplement in one tax-FREE fund.

Unlike a DI policy that your business or employer paid for, you may not have to pay income tax on your income during the time you are disabled. All of your contributions to a **Wealth Reserve**™ are FREE of tax. Your earnings may be penalty free also. Thus, there is no downside to creating and using a **Wealth Reserve**™ instead of a DI policy. Your hard-earned money is not lost to the insurer if you don't need your insurance and most of your income when you can't work will not be taxed or under penalty.

If your employer provides disability coverage, compare the benefit amount and their definition of disability. The benefits are taxable because the company paid for them. The chance of you suffering a long-term permanent disability is small. 12% of adults suffer a long-term disability, usually when they are older. The chance of a short-term disability actually decreases as you get older. In deciding how to deal with disability, keep in mind that Social Security pays a modest amount but only if your disability is total and permanent. After 24 months of benefits, you qualify for Medicare.

What policy do you need?

✓ One that defines disability as "unable to perform the duties of *your* customary occupation."
✓ Does not require total disability before partial disability payment. Allows partial pay based on your loss of income without prior total disability.
✓ Presumes loss of sight, speech, hearing, or use of limbs as total disability.
✓ Pays benefits to age 65 or for life even if you have to take

lower monthly benefit.
- ✓ Has cost-of-living rider to keep payouts current during long term coverage.
- ✓ Offers non-cancelable or guaranteed renewable (at higher premium).

If you have decided you do need a policy, the type of coverage you need is determined by your occupation. If you are self-employed and your spouse has no income, you need a policy that replaces 50% or more of your income for an extended period of time. This expense might be deductible if you own your own business.

Your benefits should begin when you can't do the duties of *your* job. If this means using your hands in a specific way, then if you can't, you should qualify. If the policy language says 'similar work,' then you won't qualify. If you travel in your job and now you can't, you want to qualify for some benefits if you can do your job without travel. You want to qualify for partial benefits even if you were not totally disabled first.

You may not be able to insure payments to age 65. This disability insurance benefit is rare. The inflation protection benefit is valuable since you may not have a claim for 20 years. Without it, your monthly amount will have half the buying power of today. Find a policy that is renewable and non-cancelable.

The language used in a 'DI' contract is important. Ask the agent or insurer what would happen in certain situations. For instance, some members have noted that a claim may be denied if the facility used for treatment has not been approved. Claims have been denied the first time through the claim process. Be persistent: See *The Rainmaker* movie for examples. You may discover how your insurer handles claims by searching the Internet for "disability claims complaints for (your insurer)."

What to avoid

- ✗ Avoid policies with "any occupation" definition. You will not qualify if you can work at any job, regardless of your prior income level. Flip burgers, answer phones?
- ✗ "Optionally renewable" or "conditionally renewable" means they can drop you anytime.
- ✗ Avoid policies that pay only for accidents, not illness; for total,

not partial *and* total disability.

If you want the peace of mind of having a guaranteed income from a disability policy, do not waste money on plans that only pay for a short period or accident-only disability. It is long-term disability that can devastate your life. Some of our members are self-employed and want their family to be secure. They buy a policy with lifetime benefits but expect to pay for the policy for only 20 years. At the same time, they accumulate enough money in their **Wealth Reserve**™ to self-insure their income after that. Investing $250 a month for 20 years may yield $250,000.

    A policy that specifies your occupation at your skill level will be more expensive but worth it, since you don't want to settle for "any" job. The policy should pay you after 90 or 180 days if you cannot work due to illness or accident. Illness is more common than accident. The policy should be 'noncan" (non cancelable) and automatically renewable.

    Avoid owning a separate credit or mortgage disability policy that pays your lender instead of you. You may be paying a higher amount for your car, credit card or mortgage loan because you agreed to carry "disability" protection when you signed up. The bank or dealer sales person often adds in the premium without explaining that you don't need this coverage for the loan. You may be paying $1,000 to $2,000 more than you have to. It is less expensive to buy one policy to pay for all your expenses should you become disabled.

How much coverage do you need?

1.   If your employer does not provide disability after your sick days are used, family members with jobs may provide enough income, especially if you have an IRA or **Wealth Reserve**™ to fall back on. Assess your family resources. Does your family income cover basic needs?
2.   Depending on your expense level, other funds or income may allow you to skip the expense of disability insurance. Determine your needs compared with the 12% chance of long-term disability from illness. Disability from accident is rare.
3.   Self-employed and small business owners may have tax advantages to help provide this essential coverage. A

comprehensive policy with the longest benefit period covers loss of earnings power. Check exclusions, pre-existing conditions restrictions and claim rules.

4. Choose optional coverage with care—"accidental total disability" is very rare—why pay for it? To decide what options and benefits you need, use the **EasySheet** below.

5. Your 'DI' benefits will be reduced by other insurance: social security, workers' compensation, veterans' benefits, union, auto, and credit disability insurance. Use one policy. Pick 3% COLA rider so your benefit stays ahead of inflation.

6. The wording of insurance policies is confusing and unclear. Ask "what would happen" if you got carpel tunnel syndrome, for instance. See "Your Rights" below and the Glossary at Insure.com/articles/disabilityinsurance/disability-terms.html

Match the policy to your lifestyle. If you have two incomes, or if one of you has coverage from work, you may not need a policy. Many members have thought through their income needs if disabled as part of their overall financial plan. Some rely on their **Wealth Reserve**™ to take advantage of its ability to cover multiple risks with one contribution.

If you have decided you need a policy, compare the amount you will spend for the protection to age 65 with the amount you could have accumulated during that time. In most cases, only self-employed professionals and small business owners can afford to pay for a policy that provides 60% of current income for years to age 65. We think even those who can afford it are still better off having the cash because most people cancel their disability policies before they use them. Insurance is not an investment.

If you are buying a policy, pick a benefit level that covers your basic expenses—housing, food, insurance, and utilities. You won't be able to save or take vacations. You can reduce spending on clothing and personal items. Again, most disability events are not total or permanent. You may be able to work part-time. Residual benefits pay an income proportional to the income you lost.

Best value

➢ Pick a policy with a benefit of 60% of salary, your "own" occupation, benefits to age 65, with 90 to 180 day waiting

"elimination" period (deductible).
➢ Non-cancelable, renewal guaranteed, with "pre-existing" condition accepted and illnesses covered.
➢ Inflation increases and partial disability options assure more benefits for the long term.

Your best value is a policy that protects your ability to provide an income for your family throughout your working life. Long-term disability is rare so many members make a plan that includes various sources of income—spouse, employer, **Wealth Reserve**™, government assistance, and home equity loan approval. Most members have two incomes and rely on their self-insurance **Wealth Reserve**™ not on a DI policy.

Self-employed members buy a policy to cover the family's sole source of income to age 65. The policy has an inflation rider to protect replacement of 60% of current income in the future. Inflation of normal proportions (3%) can rob you of half the buying power in 20 years. The policy may be deductible. The insurer's long-term solvency is a consideration so use one of the majors listed below. Make sure the policy cannot be canceled.

Small business owners may need additional options:

• Recovery benefits pay during the time you are reestablishing a customer base.
• Overhead expense pays for certain office expenses.
• Buy-out policy pays the firm to buy a disabled partner's share of the business.
• Key-person protects a firm's income from the loss due to the disability of a key employee or owner.

How and where to buy

1. Contact Guardian https://www.disabilityquotes.com/disability-insurance/diquoterequestsecure.cf ,
Unum http://www.unum.com/products/Disability/,
Insure http://www.insure.com/articles/disabilityinsurance/.
2. If you are a member of an association, fraternal or religious group, they may have discount rates.
3. If you just left your job, perhaps you can convert your old

benefits.
4. Military-related are eligible for www.USAA.com.

Compare quality products from the top 'DI' carriers. With three quotes from the top providers, you can be sure the premium provides a fair benefit when you need it.

A policy purchased through your association or group membership may be a less expensive alternative. However, check the small print for conditions if the association changes carriers. You want to use a carrier with a long-term commitment to paying benefits not paying the association.

Converting an employer group policy can be expensive but may be less expensive than an individual contract, especially if your health is in question. Some members have chosen to retire early and skip the conversion to individual coverage because the cost is too high.

The critical policy elements

◆ If policy renewal isn't guaranteed, you may not keep coverage if you get sick.
◆ Find a comfortable balance between benefit amount and lifetime coverage.
◆ If you are in good health, medical questions save you money. If not, see bad health.
◆ Select a company with financial strength of A or better.
◆ Ask for the automatic premium payment method from your credit card or bank to prevent policy lapse.

What to do if you have bad health

1. If you have a major illness, you may not obtain coverage for a re occurrence. Your association or union may offer a group policy that doesn't require tests. Carriers specialize and disability brokers will help you find one without formally being denied.
2. If you have left your job, you can convert your group policy without testing.
3. Your own business qualifies for a MET or MEWA group

coverage. Ask your Chamber of Commerce.
4. You may find it is less expensive to create your own policy. Start your <u>Wealth Reserve</u> NOW.

Use local disability income brokers to obtain bids from several specialty carriers. Your accountant or attorney may have found a reliable firm. Some professions have specialized coverage carriers. These insurers know what skills are needed for your profession and write policies for the occupation. Thus surgeons and stunt people have their own types of policies.

How carriers decide to insure you

- Sex, age, health, lifestyle, occupation, avocation, medical and family history as well as your employment, insurance, credit and driving records are used.
- Your doctor may need to give the carrier a statement. Let the doctor know you're applying.
- Choice of benefit amount and elimination period. The lower the percent of income and the longer the wait, the less expensive the policy.
- Carriers have marketing quotas to make for preferred occupations.
- Your policy should arrive 4-6 weeks after the application. Check each element.

Your Rights
1. An agent cannot modify your contract (application, endorsements and attachments). Changes must be written parts of the contract and signed by an officer.
2. Unless your misstatements are fraudulent, the policy becomes incontestable after two years. Claims cannot be denied or reduced because your condition was preexisting.
3. You have a grace period with full coverage, if your premium is late (7 days for weekly, 10 days monthly, 31 days other), unless you received non-renewal notice.
4. If a policy is lapsed, it is usually reinstated if the agent or company accepts payment, unless a re-application is required.

You're reinstated on the 45th day unless it's denied. There is a 10-day waiting period for illness coverage (none for accident).
5. You have 20 days to notify the agent or carrier of a loss.
6. The carrier has 15 days to give you the forms to prove the loss.
7. You must give written proof of loss within 90 days of the accident or disability, unless you are incapacitated. All proofs must be complete by one year.
8. Benefits are payable immediately upon receipt of proof, unless due monthly.
9. Death benefits are payable to the beneficiary or the estate of the insured. Optional: Relative can be paid up to $1,000 instead of the estate or minor beneficiary. Optional: Medical provider can be paid the benefits to facilitate payments to insured.
10. The insurer can examine you while you receive benefits or have an autopsy performed.
11. You can only sue the insurer 60 days after the loss proof is due (up to 3 years).
12. You can change the beneficiary or re-assign the benefits unless it's irrevocable.

Provisions adopted by most states

1. The agent is required to tell you about the all policy limitation before you sign.
2. You can change inaccurate medical information the www.MIB.com provides to the carrier.

Provisions insurers may include:

3. Your disability benefit may be reduced if you are employed in a more dangerous job.
4. Your benefits may be reduced if you misstate your age.
5. Your benefits cannot be increased above the company limit even with 2 policies.
6. Your benefits cannot be increased by having the same coverage from another carrier.
7. Your benefits cannot be increased by having the same

coverage from another type.
8. Your disability benefits cannot exceed your income by having 2 policies.
9. Your benefits can be reduced by the premium you owe if it is unpaid.
10. Your policy may be canceled within 5 days of notice sent unless it is non-cancelable. You receive the unused portion of the premium paid when the policy is canceled.
11. Your policy provisions must comply with your state's law no matter how written.
12. Your policy will not pay if you are engaged in illegal occupations when loss occurs.
13. Your policy will not pay if you are using alcohol or narcotics when the loss occurs.
14. Your policy may not contain a "discretionary clause" that allows the insurer to determine whether a policyholder who makes a claim is entitled to benefits.
15. Your policy must contain a definition of "disability" such as: if a person cannot perform with reasonable continuity all of the substantial and material acts required by his/her occupation, then that person is totally disabled from performing that occupation.
16. The definition of what constitutes a pre-existing condition has been substantially narrowed and clarified. A claimant must now have received treatment for a diagnosed condition in order for it to qualify as a pre-existing condition.

EasySheet: Find out if you have the best coverage and options

	Company A	Company B	Company C
Name			

Premium: __Annual __Semi __Quarter

	Company A	Company B	Company C
Individual: 2 years, 60% salary, 90 day wait	$	$	$
Individual: to age 65, 50% salary, 180 day wait	$	$	$
Self-employed professional	$	$	$
Partial allowed, "own" occupation	$	$	$
Small business group policy	$	$	$
Recovery benefit	$	$	$
Key-person disability income	$	$	$
Buy-out disabled partner	$	$	$
Residual disability	[]	[]	[]
No pre-existing limitations	[]	[]	[]
Family medical history good	[]	[]	[]
All sickness and accidents	[]	[]	[]
Good health discount	[]	[]	[]
Inflation increases	[]	[]	[]
Presumptive disability	[]	[]	[]
Non-can/guaranteed renewable	[]	[]	[]

7

The Insider's Guide to Vehicle Insurance: Beware of Double Coverage

- Your health insurance policy may cover you already, and
- You may already have towing, burial, rental car coverage, and
- Your comprehensive coverage may cost more than you can ever collect.
- Prices change frequently, so shopping can save $2,000 a year.

Un-bundle! Save up to $6,000 in 10 years

Your vehicle policy is really a <u>bundle</u> of coverage types. It includes liability protection to pay the victims of the accident for injuries and property damage, disability payments, lawsuits, and death benefits; medical and disability insurance for you and your family, protection to pay the other victims if the OTHER driver is not insured properly, legal representation if necessary, extras like towing and rental car reimbursement, money to fix your car from an accident and money to repair or replace your car if damaged by fire/theft. You may already have some of these. In some states, you have to buy coverage you don't need. Check contract terms at http://www2.iii.org/glossary/

Is it really worth learning the "tricks of the trade" and save? You bet it is! For instance, in New Jersey the same two-driver household was charged $3,600 by GE but only $1,400 by Amica, AIG, and USAA. The **$2,200 annual difference** is worth over $42,000 to you over 10 years. Your savings can pay for a home down payment or college. We advocate using a self-insurance model for your coverage. Based upon the way businesses insure themselves, the essence of this plan is to insure against catastrophic loss and use the premiums you save to build your

> **Save 30% or more**
> John of New Jersey spent 20 minutes with a call center. His premium fell 33% from $2,029.30 to $1,358 for 2 Toyotas with full coverage. The carrier is rated A++ by A.M.Best. Claims service is open 24 hours and it has the same complaint rate as State Farm in New Jersey. A year ago, he saved $567 by shopping for coverage also.

wealth. Your **Wealth Reserve**™ protects you against small losses, if any. Usually, the wealth created is greater than the losses suffered.

There are several ways to save up to 30% on your coverage and feel confident you have the proper protection. This Guide helps you buy coverage to increase your **Wealth Reserve**™. This **Wealth Reserve**™ is made up of assets that you accumulate over time so that you are self-insured. The **Wealth Reserve**™ can be used to pay higher deductibles if you should need to make a claim for a loss. The recommendations in this Guide assume that you will fund or have funded your **Wealth Reserve**™.

Each vehicle coverage category has a choice in the dollar level of protection. For instance, liability for injuries to each person can be $100,000 and 300,000 per accident. You can make your coverage expensive by picking the highest dollar limits for coverage AND picking low or ZERO deductibles. Your agent or the seller of the policy is operating with a conflict of interest: the higher premium, the greater commission. You may not need every coverage and thus save money. However, this is why the policy is sold as a bundle of different protection types.

The more you buy of what the seller recommends, the more you feel you have "good" protection. We do not think you need every item that is recommended. We help you decide what you really need without sales pressure. We provide you with a way to save money by picking high deductibles without being underinsured. The seller wants you to buy everything as presented. We help you do the **opposite:** buy only what you need.

The seller makes more when the premium is greater. The commission varies—3%-15%—and there are other incentives. The more vehicles and drivers and extras that are handled in your sales session, the larger the revenues. Sales people are trained to handle your objections, not provide you with coverage at the least cost. The same coverage can cost THREE times as much from one carrier to the next. Our checklist below lists each discount and the coverage limits that may be right for you. You can receive price quotes by phone or computer in less than 30 minutes. You can "earn" $6,000 over 10 years in just 30 minutes by asking.

This Guide helps you take advantage of our Insider's 'tricks of the trade'. You may not need some coverages. You re-direct the premium you save to your **Wealth Reserve**™. If you save $600 on your new coverage by taking the $2,500 deductible, your Reserve is over $6,000 larger in 10 years. Your **Wealth Reserve**™ is your self-insurance fund to pay the first $2,500 of a claim if you have one. The average driver files a collision claim once every three years and a comprehensive claim just once every 10 years, according to the Insurance Information Institute in New York. You will have an extra $6,500 in your **Wealth Reserve**™ by picking a higher deductible and taking the gains on the premium savings. If you don't have an accident, the $6,500 can be used to protect you against other risks.

> WARNING: This Guide offers advice on how to self-insure your risks. This Guide explains the coverage you may not need. However, before you change your coverage, make certain that the alternative plan is in place. Do not drop any coverage before you check your alternative insurer. Start your self-insurance **Wealth Reserve**™.

Let's talk about the health portion of your car policy. If your family has medical coverage, there is no need to pay for coverage again, year after year. If you drop the policy's personal-injury protection (PIP), redirect the savings to your **Wealth Reserve**™. Your insurer may ask you to provide the name and number of your health insurance policy. Make sure your medical coverage is the comprehensive type so that if you need massive surgery after an accident, you are taken care of. Check our Insider's Guide to Health Insurance. Make sure you have a plan for income if you are disabled by an accident. Our Insider's Guide to Disability Insurance explains how members use their **Wealth Reserve**™ to cover this risk. Usually, separate Accident and Dismemberment coverage are not needed.

If you have a plan to pay final expenses and replace family income, you don't need to pay for funeral coverage again, year after year. Add the savings to your **Wealth Reserve**™ as our members illustrate in our Insider's Guide to Life Insurance. If you have a plan to pay for road emergencies and rental car reimbursement, you don't need to pay for coverage again, year after year. Our Guides can help you set-up a plan to cover each risk.

Your "preferred driver" status may qualify you for "super preferred" rates. Careful drivers can save extra premium by not making claims for small repairs. Most insurers credit you for not having accidents too.

Buy only the protection you need

This Guide helps you learn which coverages you don't need. In a sentence, you can save money by paying the smaller claims yourself and buying enough liability protection to prevent a catastrophic loss of life and all your assets. The first line of defense is to protect your family with a safe car and safe driving habits. The second is 'lawsuit' insurance.

You may qualify for "preferred" or top-tier rates if you have strong driving and credit behavior. Ask the insurer to give you the best rates based upon the insurer's underwriting experience with your profile and lifestyle. Whatever information you provide to an insurer is supplemented by many informational sources that should agree. Don't lie. The carrier will just downgrade your claim payout to match the facts they find later. When you have a large claim, you don't want to delay payment because the insurer must investigate a misleading statement on your application.

Carriers have many discounts, up to 30%, but YOU HAVE TO ASK FOR EACH ONE. Use the **EasySheet below** to go through the list. If you are a responsible driver, you may be subsidizing poor drivers. In a study by Qualityplanning.com, it was determined that:

"Rating error introduces significant inequalities into auto insurance; honest people subsidize the dishonest, low risk drivers subsidize high risk drivers, those that rarely use their vehicles subsidize high-mileage drivers."

Make sure your family is in the correct tier with an insurer that values low-risk lifestyles. For instance, many carriers rate drivers by only two annual mileage categories—zero to 7,500 miles and over 7,500 miles. Few carriers charge extra for SUVs that are expensive to repair. Most people are paying more than they need to —over $950 extra in Atlanta, for instance—according to a 2003 survey by Progressive. See http://articles.chicagotribune.com/2013-01-28/business/chi-consumer-group-finds-rich-likely-to-pay-less-for-car-insurance-20130128_1_auto-insurers-safe-driver-state-farm

Pick the coverage that protects your lifestyle

Save your assets. Buy the maximum liability coverage: Protect your assets from a lawsuit that could wipe you out. Buy an additional policy called an "umbrella" or excess liability to cover legal fees and court costs. If you loose, this policy will pay the judgment. You will not have to sell your home or business. Find coverage with The Insider's Guide to "Lawsuit" Insurance.

Save **30%**. Drop the personal-injury protection (PIP) if you have comprehensive medical coverage and a disability income plan and life insurance on the wage-earners in your household. If you or your family members are involved in an accident, your personal health insurance will be the primary payer. Ask your insurer if you really need uninsured motorist protection. Buy the least amount you can if PIP is required by law.

Save **30%**. Drop the collision and comprehensive if your vehicle is over 5 years old and no loan is outstanding. The cost of collision and comprehensive coverage may actually exceed the depreciated value, if the car is "totaled." Invest the savings for a luxury car at 40% off with our The Insider's Guide to Vehicle Purchase.

Save **30%**. Raise the deductible to the maximum for collision and comprehensive if the vehicle has a loan outstanding. Confirm that your **Wealth Reserve**™ covers the deductible. New cars loose value so fast, "Gap" insurance is sold to pay the balance owed to your lender if a new vehicle is "totaled." This is the dealer's highest profit margin product because it is rarely needed. Have a plan to cover the loan. This is why many independent people buy 3-year old luxury cars instead of new ones.

The wording of insurance policies is confusing and unclear. Ask your insurer "what would happen" in a hypothetical situation. Give the details of an imaginary accident and see how your carrier would handle it. Ask for an explanation of every phase of the claim process—who to call, who estimates damage, who repairs, who defends you if sued, who arbitrates disputes. Ask if there is an ombudsman. Assemble an accident-report package for your glove box so that you are always prepared. docudentusa.com/

Save **15%**. Drop the duplicates, like road service and rental car reimbursement if you already receive these benefits or have a plan. If you have an accident, your credit card emergency operator (VISA, MC, AMEX) will call you a towing service. Determine in advance where the vehicle will go for repairs. What other transport is available during repairs?

Save **30%**. Ask for every discount the insurer has available. Go through the list with the insurer. Confirm you have the best rate-tier for your demographic profile (female, 39, ZIP code, garaged, no accident, non-drinker, etc).

Find the BEST value based upon your lifestyle

✓ "Direct writers" don't have the expense of agents and fancy buildings.
✓ Some insurers are trying to become more competitive but only 1/3 of drivers shop around.

This Guide helps you protect your family and assets from catastrophic loss. Your **Wealth Reserve**™ is your "self-insurance" fund built by investing what you save in premiums from eliminating duplicate coverages. Carriers usually keep that extra premium as profit. Insurers benefit from the fact that most drivers don't check the price of coverage for their needs. Most drivers think they receive "preferred" rates and service, even though safe drivers don't receive automatic rate reductions. Safe drivers actually keep insurers profitable. There is fraud and mismanagement in the industry. Only recently have GEICO and Progressive challenged the market leaders State Farm and Allstate. Recent surveys suggest that the average driver is overpaying by $500 to $1,000. In 10 years, that's $5,000 to $10,000 for your other insurance needs.

The industry is changing. Each insurer acts on a strategy they think will be profitable this year. This means that your insurer may no longer think you are a profitable "segment." You change too. You may now fit into another insurer's niche. We can't know which insurer will offer you the best value TODAY. The Internet has made shopping easier. We know that most financially-independent people have found better value for their money from insurers that focus on them—not on their salespeople. We think that the industry should provide better service for less. The industry calls these insurers, "direct writers." They have fewer expenses. You can usually pay less for the coverage you need by confirming how you drive.

One of the best-known insurers that deal directly with you is Amica. Amica.com prides itself on providing award-winning service. It has won the J. D. Power service quality award for many years. Customers are loyal for another reason. Amica is a mutual company. They insure safe drivers so they pay *you* for driving well. Quick claim settlement should be the goal of any vehicle insurer. Amica has one of the highest customer retention rates.

When price is the important criterion for you, a safe driver, you can benefit by shopping GEICO, Progressive and other insurers on a regular basis. The Internet can speed your shopping. We think that this method will replace the old way of buying financial services. Independents want good value, not 'good hands.' Until there is a carrier which offers coverage specifically for the self-insured customer, shopping is the best way to buy.

Because some insurers specialize, the best value for you may be the carrier which provides you with special benefits due to your occupation, associations, or situation. There are many insurers that understand their specific customers better than others and so provide benefits you may find valuable. For example, USAA provides coverage for those with military service. USAA.com has no agents or offices, yet provides such good service that the insurance industry uses it as it's "best-in-class" model of processing and service excellence. It was named '**Best**' by *Worth* magazine readers.

This Guide helps you take advantage of our insider's 'tricks of the trade.'

Other special carriers are listed at the end of this chapter. Progressive has taken the lead in aggressive underwriting styles. For instance, it tested rates based on miles driven. Electric Insurance has found union workers to be its niche, while New Jersey Manufacturers has focused on the employees of the state's employers and government.

AIG took advantage of the lack of new underwriters in New

Jersey in 2000 to increase market share. In Massachusetts, carriers offer Group Discounts to employers. Many direct-to-customer insurers make it easy to interact with them in the way that *you*, not your agent, find convenient. You can shop by phone or Internet in less than 30 minutes. If you have a claim, you can begin the process at the accident site.

Shop every two years

✓ Shop for the best price by going directly to the consumer-focused carriers: Amica.com. (**800.242.6422**), Geico.com (**800.861.8380**), Progressive.com (**800.776.4737**), 21st.com (**877.310.5687**), ElectricInsurance.com (**800.342.5342**), Response.com (**800.518.2984**). Veterans: USAA.com (**800-531-8080**).

✓ Members have found that comparing prices periodically can save them $500 to $1,000: CarInsurance.com/, Insurance.com

✓ Check your state for lists through NAIC.org.

Compare price and service, just like you would shop for new cell phone. Insurers see you very differently from year to year. One carrier might see you as a low-risk driver. Another might see you as a way to boost market share. Another might put you in a general pool for all drivers from your state with no discount for good driving or high credit scores. Your agent is motivated to use carriers with higher premium rates for commission and incentive purposes. On the other hand, an agent may be the only way you can find an insurer that covers you. You won't know until you shop: Use the EasySheet below.

Many insurers use **insurance scores** to help set your premium. They claim that the way you handle financial matters predicts your claim behavior. Many states have allowed carriers to use scores as long as certain restrictions are honored. One insurer suspends using the score if you experience the following life-altering events:

- Death of spouse or close family member
- Divorce
- Identity theft
- Major illness or injury
- Recent loss of a job

This method of evaluating financial responsibility is designed to look at a driver's long-term track record of handling money. Low- and moderate-income drivers do not automatically fare worse than high-income drivers, according to the insurer. This insurer looks at a person's bill-paying practices over a seven-year period, with greater weight given to the last three years.

Critical policy elements

1. Select a company with at least an "A" rating. Only 5% have A++.
2. Select annual policy renewal, if available, to protect you from mid-year rate hikes.
3. If you're concerned about service, **Amica** Erie Shelter NJ Manufacturers and **USAA** have very high customer loyalty.
4. Customer "complaint ratios" indicate quality. For example, in New Jersey, Manufacturers' complaint rate is very low and Mercury is high. Check NAIC.org for your state's data.
5. Confirm you have been placed in the best risk classification possible.
6. Confirm you have all possible carrier discounts. See the **EasySheet** below.

Driving record not perfect?

If you have high rates or have had trouble obtaining coverage, find out why. Your best strategy may be to become 'hidden' in a group. Your union, employer or association may have a relationship with an insurer that provides for group rates. Carriers benefit from the fact that the group members have certain positive characteristics. For instance, insurers in Massachusetts underwrite employer groups. You can avoid individual underwriting that may raise your premium.

Another way to find coverage at a reasonable price is by using an experienced independent agent. If you have coverage for your home from one of the larger carriers, your vehicle coverage might be accepted. Your agent may have a good reputation with a certain underwriter and thus add your policy to the agency.

There are other insurers that specialize in high risk groups or vehicles. See the list of carriers at the end of this Guide. Members of the medical community may find discounted coverage at AMAinsure.com. The legal profession has a special relationship at abiins.com/. You may find that a small carrier using aggressive underwriting through an Internet portal is just right for your needs. Most carriers offer quotes on their Internet site.

Finally, your state may have a high-risk 'pool' that allows carriers to charge the maximum possible for your coverage. Many city storefront insurance agencies exist to find coverage for first-time buyers. Keeping a clean record for three years may help you jump out of the risk 'pool'. Your state may also offer assistance in finding insurance. Check naic.org for your state's insurance department site. Some states offer help in buying a basic policy to encourage those who drive without insurance. It is not clear whether the state can eliminate uninsured drivers by running these programs. California's pilot test has not been an overwhelming success.

How carriers decide to insure you

1. Your age, occupation, education level, vehicle type, driver record, credit history, zip code, use, garage, drive distance, and marital statuses are the factors. Safe car? See iihs.org
2. Repair costs iihs.org/brochures/ictl/ictl.html.
3. Your carrier uses your insurance, credit and driving records. MIB.com
4. Some use the length of time with the company, other policies, and your skills.
5. Vehicles are rated by safety, cost of repair, theft record and equipment.
6. Choice of deductible: Large claims are preferred to many small claims.
7. Carriers may market to you as a niche or as a geographical strategy.
8. California requires insurers to rate you by your driving record not your zip code. USAA dropped rates.

What to do if you are declined, non-renewed or dropped

Many insurers use modern marketing methods and models to run their businesses now. The models may tell them to drop you individually or as a group because you have a profile they do not want. Carriers look to "professional" marketers and "data-mining" experts to find you or drop you or not pay claims. Allstate is accused of denying legitimate benefits using a McKinsey management system. Businessweek.com 5/1/6

One of our New Jersey members was dumped by the insurer associated with AAA. The member has a very good credit rating and driving record—one of the two drivers (over 40 years old) was rear-ended 5 years before. Guess what the carrier said about the 'non-renewal'?

AAA's insurer said that their "computer model" decided that our member was "due" for an accident and they were dropping the customer of 10 years, now, before the claim!! We helped the member file a complaint with the state's insurance regulator. We helped the member go shopping for a new carrier. The member found a carrier that charged much less. Sweet revenge: AAA's carrier was forced to reinstate the member and was fined by the state.

A year later, the member went shopping again for coverage. This time they answered an advertisement from another company with an A++ rating. They obtained coverage—same limits and guarantees on two vehicles—but for another savings of about 30%. The new carrier had just entered the New Jersey market and needed good customers. Our member learned that they can save by shopping for new insurance on a regular basis just like cell phone service. Today, most agency-focused companies are trying to maximize profits; not looking for a long-term relationship. (The NJ member has still not had an accident after 31 years.)

You may have difficulty finding insurance because of the type of vehicle you use. A recent survey by Runzheimer International found these expensive cars are hard to insure: Ford Mustang convertible, Honda S2000 convertible, Chrysler Sebring, Toyota Celica GTS, Mitsubishi Eclipse Spyder GTS convertible, Dodge Neon SRT-4, VW Passat W8, Honda Civic Hatchback, Subaru Impreza WRX AWD Turbo, and Volkswagen GTI VR6.

At the other end of the cost spectrum is: Saturn Ion, Saturn L300, Chevy Aveo, Chevy Colorado, Ford Escape XLS, Mazda 3,

Dodge Caravan, Honda Accord DX, Hyundai Santa Fe, and Toyota Corolla.

If you are declined by the insurer, you need to find out why. There are some things you can do about it and some you can't. If you've made too many claims or have too many speeding tickets, you need to take advantage of some of the relationships you already have so that you can be included as an affinity group member. This includes social and professional associations. For instance, if you are a legal worker, you can use the abiins.com/ site. In Massachusetts, there are a number of associations which have received discount group rates from certain carriers.

Claim process

Use an accident reporting package like those at wreckit.com while you wait for the police. Obtain witness names and numbers. Take pictures of the scene, not the other driver. Say little beyond your name and insurance info. You want to provide little for the other person's lawyer to 'hang' you with. Call your carrier. Get a copy of the police report. Forward all items to the claim's department ASAP. Follow up weekly. Get the processor's name. Be nice. Expect the best, be prepared for the worst. Make copies and notes of all events.

If your accident settlement is not fair, ask for the insurer ombudsman or review committee for a hearing. Present your evidence: "**Just the facts, Ma'am, just the facts**." Ask an experienced insurance attorney if it is worth pursuing.

Carriers specialize

1. New and teen drivers: Sentry.com 800-3SENTRY, Progressive.com 800-776-4737, statefarm.com, Experienced agent
2. Motorcycles: Progressive.com 800-776-4737, Guideone.com 877-448-4331
3. Exotic: Americancollectors.com 800-360-2277
4. Veterans: USAA.com 800-531-8080, AFI.org 800-495-8234
5. Federal employees: GEICO.com 800-861-8380
6. Students and educators: GEICO.com 800-861-8380, Lancer-ins.com 800-782-8902, horacemann.com/ 800-999-1030
7. USPS, VFW, GM: GEICO.com 800-861-8380.
8. Overseas drivers: GEICO.com 800-861-8380, chartisinsurance.com/
9. No accident drivers: Amica.com, 800-242-6422,
10. Homeowners: 21st.com/ 800-314-9947
11. Nondrinkers: Guideone.com 877-448-4331
12. Agricultural and rural: Farmbureau.com 877/860-2904
13. Fifth-wheels, RV, Motor homes, Travel trailers: Foremost.com 800-752-2461, Rv-insurance.com 800-400-0186
14. AARP member: TheHartford.com 888-808-5254
15. Religious orgs: Gideone.com 877-448-4331
16. Retail Hardware: Sentry.com 800-3SENTRY
17. Union and GE employees: ElectricInsurance.com 800-227-2757
18. Florida, Thegeneral.com 877-GENERAL,
19. Massachusetts drivers: Mass.gov 617-521-7794
20. New Jersey drivers: 21st.com/ 800-314-9547, IFAauto.com 877-432-2277, Njcure.com/ 800-535-CURE, Manufacturers njm.com 800-232-6600, plymouthrocknj.com/ 800.516.9242
21. Special transport vehicles: Northlandins.com 800-237-9334
22. Business: Chubb.com 800-36-CHUBB, Lancer-ins.com 800-782-8902
23. California drivers: 21st.com 800-211-SAVE, Thegeneral.com 877-GENERAL
24. Medical: AMAinsure.com 877-310-5687
25. Legal: abiins.com/ 800-532-9490
26. Alabama, Georgia and Mississippi drivers: alfains.com
27. Teachers: Response.com 800.518.2984, HoraceMann.com 800-999-1030
28. Churchgoers: Gideone.com 877-448-4331
29. Golf carts: Progressive.com 800-776-4737

Check state insurance department NAIC.org for auto rates by location by type of driver. Example: NJ state.nj.us/cgi-bin/dobi/autopremiums/ziplist.pl.

EasySheet: Shop for the best coverage and discounts
http://www2.iii.org/glossary/

	Company A	Company B	Company C
Name			

Premium: Annual__ Semi__ Quarter__

	Company A	Company B	Company C
Liability Coverage (required)	$	$	$
Bodily injury to others	$	$	$
Property damage to others	$	$	$
Medical Expenses (duplicated?)	$	$	$
Uninsured Coverage (required?)	$	$	$
Collision (crash damage)?			
High deductible or Drop	$	$	$
Comprehensive (theft/vandalism)?			
High deductible or Drop	$	$	$
Grand Total	$	$	$

Ask for discounts:

	Company A	Company B	Company C
Multi-car	__	__	__
Multi-policy	__	__	__
Carpooling or limited driving	__	__	__
Good driver	__	__	__
Age 10% after age 55	__	__	__
Loyalty 10% after 6 years	__	__	__
Good driver	__	__	__
Defensive driving course	__	__	__
Driver's education	__	__	__
Good student	__	__	__
College student not driving	__	__	__
Anti-lock brakes	__	__	__
Anti-theft devices	__	__	__
Air bag/automatic seat belt	__	__	__
Safe vehicle like Camry	__	__	__
Affinity group membership	__	__	__
Other _____	__	__	__

Protect your assets from suits:
Umbrella personal liability coverage
   $1,000,000 Protection $ $ $

8

The Insider's Guide to Life Insurance: Do you need it?

Only if . . .

- ✓ Your family members depend on your earned income, or
- ✓ Your business asset needs to be divided among heirs, or
- ✓ You wish to leave a legacy, tax-**FREE**.

Save $20,000 over your lifetime

Single folks with no dependents don't need coverage. Quite a few people **don't need** life insurance, despite the industry hype. Consider who relies on you for support. If others don't depend on your paycheck or assets, you may not need coverage. Agents like to say that young people need insurance to protect their insurability for later life. Truth is, almost everyone can find a policy when they need one. New underwriting guidelines have lowered rates for everyone in the last 10 years. A 50-year-old can buy coverage for about $1 a day. Even those with chronic illness can find coverage if necessary. Your personal debts die with you.

You don't need coverage if your assets are large enough to protect your dependents. If you have accumulated enough assets to generate supplemental income, you don't need insurance to replace your income.

> **Example of saving up to 30%**: John of N.J. needed term coverage. He spent 30 minutes with a call center representative at 1-800-555-4655 and had the underwriting tests. The new 10-year $200,000 policy cost fell 26% to $356, even though John is now 51 years old. The new carrier is rated "A+" by A.M.Best. John now pays 26% less and he is 5 years older. Rates fell.

Confirm that your family could continue living on your assets if you were not around. While you are accumulating assets, a combination of assets and **term life** insurance coverage protects your family. Eventually the power of compounding enables your assets to grow to a level that you don't need insurance to replace income any longer. You save the cost of the premiums.

As the cost of term insurance rises with your age, the **level** of coverage you need to buy may be **reduced** because your other assets have grown. The assets take the place of insurance as far as replacing your income for your family is concerned. Members have found that by age 50, they need greater retirement assets than they need insurance to protect their income for family members.

One member was paying $312 a month for life insurance but his kids were grown and he was divorced. After 20 years of military service, he had little invested for retirement. He dropped his insurance and began buying assets that "grow by themselves". He downloaded the application and began the automatic accumulation of his **Wealth Reserve**™ of $1,000,000. Together with the $312 savings from the life insurance, he saved another $188 per month on his vehicle, health and disability insurance policies using our Guides. Investing the total $500 per month, he will now be able to accomplish his financial goals with his new wife. She has her own income and assets.

What type do you need?

- ✓ Your employer's policy ends if you leave your employer.
- ✓ An immediate legacy for your heirs can be purchased with one premium when you have non-liquid assets.
- ✓ Your business may deduct the cost of a policy on your life.

Individual 10- or 20-year level term insurance is so inexpensive today that almost everyone under age 50 can afford it—$500,000 may cost $30 a month. Since employment is becoming more discontinuous, self-insurance has replaced permanent coverage as the financial reality of an independent lifestyle. Buying coverage in the 21st century must be viewed as insuring your own **ability to produce income** and buy assets to protect your family, no matter where you work. If your financial goals include becoming independent, then at least 10% of your income must go to buying assets that "grow by themselves," not buying insurance.

By the time you have accumulated sufficient assets to produce income, you will not need death insurance. Example: In just 20 years, with assets of $500,000, your family could receive an income of $40,000 per year. Life insurance would be a waste of money if you had the assets to live on. Our insurance company Insider explained how this works for his friends Fred and Susan in a previous chapter.

Since most of us don't have $500,000 in assets when we begin a family, we need a way to recreate our income if we die. Term insurance provides that bridge between the time we don't have the assets and the time we do. Coverage other than term is not needed. In fact, using our family protection dollars for anything other than term insurance means not buying assets that "grow by themselves" and not having $1 million later. This is such a waste of hard-earned income. The insurer gets the use of your money's earnings not you.

Without the assets, we won't be able to protect ourselves or our family from job loss, disability, extended sickness, premature death, or insufficient retirement funds. It is too expensive to buy insurance for all the things that might go wrong. Having a Self-Insurance **Wealth Reserve**™ provides the best protection for all family needs. You are self-insured with assets that grow by themselves but can be sold to pay for any of life's challenges.

If you are over age 65 and have sufficient assets to provide for your family, you can use some of your assets to set up a tax-FREE lump-sum to your heirs. One of the benefits of life insurance is the creation of an **immediate legacy** outside your will. A single premium can provide a set benefit for family or charity. Unlike an annuity, the benefit is a tax-FREE and immediate windfall. We detail the alternatives in our Insider's Guide to Wealth Transfer.

If you are a business owner, insurance benefits can be used to provide the cash to distribute ownership of the business or its equivalent so heirs can be satisfied. Insurance can be used to help the business overcome the loss of important contributors to the business. Life insurance can be used to fund employee benefits. Our Insider's Guides can help you find the right plan and insurer for your needs. www.TheInsidersGuides.com

What to avoid

- ✓ Credit and mortgage life. Buy one term policy to cover all joint debts and replace your income.
- ✓ Policies sold by agents from brand-name firms—MetLIfe, NYLife, Prudential, etc—are the most expensive.

- ✓ Applications with a few questions. You could pay 10 times more than you should. Questions and tests <u>reduce</u> the price.
- ✓ Permanent or Whole or Universal life.

Half of all cash value policies are canceled within 5 years. <u>There is no refund</u>. Coverage of $250,000 costs an average of $3,220 per year for life! Your **Wealth Reserve**™ becomes $250,000 in 20 years and you don't need to die to use it. There are many names for these permanent policies: See <u>Stop wasting $3,000 every year: 101 Financial Products Not to buy</u>.

You have probably guessed which types of insurance our members buy. Any plan that is sold by a sales person which has a savings or investing component is

> we are more likely to outlive our savings than to die prematurely. 1/3 of Americans have $0 net worth.

wasting your hard-earned income. Before low-cost mutual funds existed, these plans may have been useful. Not any more.

Example: MetLife charged $983 for the same $300,000 30-year **term policy** as SBLI provided for $384. Their financial strength ratings are A+ and their underwriting requirements are the same. The difference, $599, over 30 years is $17,970. If invested, this difference can add $175,000 to YOUR assets when you need them. The SHOCKER: the median net worth of a 33-year-old American is just $8,525 including home and car! Build YOUR assets; not theirs! Compare at:
http://cgi.money.cnn.com/tools/networth_ageincome/

If you need term coverage later in life, shopping is crucial. Prices range from $15 to $345 per month for $500,000 benefit for a 38-year-old female. It depends on your health, family history, lifestyle and the insurer's commissions.

Also, any plan that covers a small part of your overall need is expensive because the more coverage you buy at one time, the cheaper each $1,000 of coverage will be. Any plan that promises to give you your premium back if you don't die is obviously charging you too much. Instead, invest the extra charge yourself.

Insurance plans that do **NOT** require medical tests are overcharging you. If you are healthy, you will be paying for everyone else who is not. Also, you do not need to waste your protection dollars on insurance for each loan separately. Besides, your heirs may need to keep the mortgage loan to save on taxes.

You can purchase or add to a mutual fund with automatic investments to pay for your final expenses instead of an expensive funeral policy. Funeral policy providers may not be around for you.

Insurance plans that cover children are shamefully exploitative. Do you really want to benefit from your child's death? These policies seem cheap to loving grandparents but the money could be buying assets that "grow by themselves" in a college or first home **Wealth Reserve**™ for the child.

If you already own a non-term life policy, think about your options to stop paying for it. Don't borrow from an old policy to buy a new one. You are just paying the commission again. An old policy may be paid up already. Ask the carrier for options. If you don't need the cash value in the policy as income now, you can convert the policy to an immediate income stream. You can direct the payments to buy a tax-FREE **Wealth Reserve**™ for your own security or your heirs. Investors may buy a retiree's policy if not needed. We provide options in our <u>Insider's Guide to Wealth Transfer</u>.

How much coverage to keep?

You should own just enough coverage to meet your needs now and invest the rest in your self-insurance **Wealth Reserve**™. To find exactly how much you need now, use our **EasySheet** below. Your needs change every decade or so, so check it every time you experience a life-changing event: job, marriage, kids, house, business, education, divorce, pre-retirement, elder care, etc.

✓ If your family members depend on your income, determine how many years they need to receive your net pay. Your spouse may have a career and need only 2 years to adjust to your death. If your spouse does not have a career, use 4-6 years of pay. Add 1-2 years for each young child. Your assets may cover the need.

✓ If you have debts—mortgage, vehicles, credit cards, medical, other—that you want paid off, estimate the total debt, including loans covered by credit insurance. Cancel the credit and mortgage life insurance after you buy a new term policy.

✓ Subtract your income-producing assets—properties, securities, savings and pensions.

✓ Subtract your current life insurance amounts. The balance is the amount you need today. If you rely on the policy you may receive at work, that coverage will end if you leave your employer. That is not the best time to look for coverage. This balance does not include amounts for spouse retirement. Your spouse may need to use our Insider's Guide to Retirement Plans to have enough from your policy benefit for retirement. The amount of coverage usually represents a transition not a windfall to your family.

Best value

- ✓ 10- or 20-year level-premium term policy locks in your rate without the extra reserves cost. Avoid 30-year's costs—buy THREE 10-year contracts.
- ✓ Term insurance is priced in increments of $50,000. You're likely to pay more for $160,000 than for $200,000, so obtain quotes for "rounded-up" amounts.
- ✓ You can reduce coverage later if you don't need it: Check evaluatelifeinsurance.org.

We think your **best value** is 10- or 20-year level term insurance. If you are in good health, you can buy a $500,000 benefit for about $1 per day even if you are age 50. At age 35, the cost is about $155 annually. The cost is level for 10 years. If you need more or less coverage for another 10 years, your rate will probably be **lower** because people are living longer. Rates begin to climb at age 50 so lock in your rate for 10 years by then. By age 60, you probably don't need coverage because you have assets to cover future income needs. If you don't, see our Insider's Guide to Retirement Spending to insure you have enough for the rest of your life.

The 10- or 20-year level term is the best value because you are not paying extra premium for the reserves required for longer terms of coverage. (This reserve is called "XXX" believe it or not.) The Return of Premium ROP term adds another 150% to the cost just so the agent can say that you will get your premium back if you don't die. Skip it; the cost of inflation works against you.

If you receive term insurance as an **employee benefit**, compare the price for your own policy. If your spouse is not employed, having an individual policy provides positive security. If you become unemployed, your coverage will terminate. It is easier and cheaper to buy insurance when you don't need it—when you are healthy and employed. If your spouse is employed, the need for insurance to replace your income is less. The same applies to your spouse's situation. The amount of coverage to buy will probably be less if your employer also provides a term policy free.

One of our members, an executive at a large company, received three times his earnings in life insurance. This amount would be paid to his spouse in addition to any other benefits at death. His spouse was employed and our member felt the amount from the company would be enough to help her make the transition. They had other assets so he did not buy more insurance.

However, in the late 90s, the company experienced some problems and cut some of the employees' benefits, including the life insurance. Concurrently, our member developed some medical problems. When he went to buy his first term policy at age 46, he was faced with paying triple the price for his policy. His medical condition was cause for part of the increase. Another part was attributed to the need for a longer-term policy. Now that he had a medical history, he felt his rates would only go up if he purchased only a 10-year term then. He decided to buy a 20-year term policy.

We recommend that you buy 10-year term insurance as you would any commodity—on price alone. A 20-year term can be just $10 more at younger ages. A term policy without any extras will cost the same each year and pay the benefit if you die. There is no reason to pay more than you have to. Some insurers price their term to attract new customers. Some price the product as a "loss leader" or convenience to their agent's clients. Some price the product to provide a healthy commission to the salesperson. For your age and health, you can find the least expensive policy online or by phone in minutes.

When carriers underwrite your life, they price the policy for accidental death in your early years. The typical $500,000 coverage costs about $15 a month from age 30 to 40. At 45, coverage is $30 and at 50, $40 a month. After 50 years, people die from diseases more often than accidents, so you pay less if you prove your good health. Best rates are $57 at age 55 for 10 years. You might need less coverage because your assets help make you self-insured. Some members reduce their policy amount by half or drop it altogether by age 55.

The industry uses super-low rates in advertising. They want

only the healthiest persons. Others use rates more in line with your actual health, called "standard" risk. Your health may not be perfect at age 50 but you can find the least expensive price for your condition by knowing the insider's "tricks of the trade." For instance, your weight needs to be under 203 pounds if you are a 6 foot tall male. Some carriers allow a little more weight but the trick is to know what a healthy weight is for your size. Ask your doctor.

Other criteria they use are:

- Family history: your parents and sibs must have no history of cardiovascular disease or cancer BEFORE age 60.
- Smoking: you cannot use tobacco in the last 5 years. There are some insurers that accept cigars but you have to prove it.
- Health: you cannot have a life-threatening condition.
- Cholesterol: numbers under 210 are accepted for the best price. The good-to-bad ratio must be 4.5-5. One firm will allow medication to control the problem for low rates.
- Blood pressure: you cannot have a history. At age 40, best price cut-offs are 130/80, 135/80 and 140/85.
- Driving drunk: you can't have a history in the last 5 years. More than one moving violation is cause for concern for some insurers.
- Travel: visiting dangerous areas (as defined by the State Department) is not in the profile of low risk folks.
- Extreme sports: racing, diving, jumping, climbing can kill you.
- If your health is good, use the Internet to buy the cheapest policy among many carriers. See below.

If you have health concerns, we suggest you use a knowledgeable professional who sells multi-company term for a living. They "place" policies with the insurer which is right for your condition. If you keep applying at different insurers, looking for a lower rate, the history of repeated applications and "ratings" are accumulated by the industry risk database, called the MIB.com. Carriers assume that if you apply more than once, you must be ready to die and are buying every policy you can. They are unlikely to give you their best rate. An experienced agent determines a rate before applying or some web sites provide the underwriting information.

How and where to buy

✓ If you want a knowledgeable professional to help you, contact ameritasdirect.com/ (**800-555-4655**), USAA.com (**800-365-8722**), SBLI.com (**888-438-7254**), Amica.com (**800-234-5433**) or AccuQuote.com (**800-442-9899**). Spanish option: Masterquote.com (**800-337-5433**) .
✓ If you are healthy go for the **lowest price** among quality carriers, contact Insure.com (**800-995-9790**) or selectquote.com/Your bank may offer policies without fluids tests. These policies cost much more for less coverage. If you are in good health, save 50% or more, and get the health "check-up" FREE.

It usually takes about 30 minutes to find and complete the application for a low-cost term policy. You don't need the extra cost riders like "premium-refund" coverage or accidental death. You can get the quote and application on the Internet or by phone. If you have completed the **EasySheet**, you know how much coverage you really need at this time.

The price has declined over the last 40 years so you save by buying a <u>new</u> 10-year policy each period. If you buy a 30-year term, you pay extra for carrier reserves. Insure.com and Insuranceclick.com guarantee that you will see the lowest-price. Some Internet services are just agent lead providers and don't quote the prices. If the site doesn't show a quote from low-cost leader, SBLI, move on. One member saved 26% over his previous 10-year policy of $200,000 coverage even though he is older now.

Another member also saved but he actually needed less coverage. He is now 56 and does not fit the weight limit for his height so he is now classified as "standard" not "preferred." He only needs $250,000 for 10 years because he will have enough assets to self-insure his family by then. He is on track to have over $1 million for retirement spending. He used savings from our Guides to pay for it.

If your health has failed by the time you renew, almost every policy sold through the sites mentioned here will renew at higher rates. But it is wise to ask an experienced term agent to find a policy that suits your condition. The renewal rates from some low-priced carriers are horrific because they don't want to be in that age market. Most people drop their coverage before dying of natural causes so the insurer always wins.

One member was trying to obtain life insurance. He was HIV positive. Most insurers will not provide coverage even though recent treatments are more effective than in the past. Our Insider suggested that since treatments seem to working for the member, investing $3000 per year in a market index fund would provide the largest benefit of a legacy to the family as possible. The fund would pass tax-free ("stepped up" basis) at death just like life insurance. See The Insider's Guide to Wealth Transfer.

The critical policy elements

- If you are in good health, medical tests save you money.
- Confirm the insurer has high financial strength ratings ("A" or better) and low complaint ratio and complaint type at https://eapps.naic.org/cis/.
- If policy renewal isn't guaranteed, you may not get coverage if you get really sick.
- If your beneficiary is other than your spouse, compare it to your will. The backup person (contingent or secondary) should be your children's guardian, named in your will, in case you and your spouse die together. Never name minors or estates: the money will go to lawyers and the courts.
- Automatic premium payments from your credit card or bank account will ensure that the policy will not lapse even though carriers charge extra for this convenience.

What to do if you have bad health

✓ If you have been treated for a major illness in the past 10 years, you may not be classified as *preferred* or *standard*, but you may still save on your coverage. Carriers specialize and experienced people will find the right one.
✓ Your association or union may offer a group policy that doesn't require tests. The amount of insurance is usually minimal.
✓ Masterquote.com (**800-337-5433**) specializes in policies for

those who have health problems.

Insurance professionals can find a policy for you, no matter what medical condition or social situation you are in. These specialists may earn up to 100% of the first year premium but it is worth it long term. There are carriers that offer policies for "impaired risk" conditions, as they are called.

For instance, a carrier with experience insuring people with certain cancers can provide some benefits. There are agents that specialize in this area. They can help you find coverage without jeopardizing your chances by being declined by inappropriate carriers.

We recommend that you self-insure your risk using our strategy in Chapter 4 to have enough to meet your goals. Compare the accumulation value of the amount you must pay for premiums. If the premium for $150,000 permanent coverage is $2000 a year for 20 years, investing could produce $150,000 or more and you could use for a retirement supplement if needed.

How carriers decide to insure

1. Medical tests indicate your level of risk above or below normal life expectancy.
2. Your carrier checks your insurance (MIB.com), credit (myfico.com) and driving records (choicetrust.com).
3. The contestability period protects the carrier against deliberate misrepresentation. During this two year period, the carrier can cancel coverage.
4. Your doctor may need to give the carrier a statement. Let the doctor know you have applied for insurance.
5. Your policy should arrive 4-6 weeks after the tests. Check each element of the policy for accuracy and conditions.

Carriers don't like to lose money so they use disease and death tables to charge you the same price as all others with the same conditions. If each person is in the correct group of risk level, every person's family receives their death benefit and the company makes money from the investment of premiums. If you have provided inaccurate information, the tests and database usually catch you. If not, the benefit will not be paid in the first two years.

The record usually shows you lied. Life insurance works for people who are in good health and die prematurely. It doesn't work as a lottery for you. It works for the insurers; holding $1 billion.

Beware of the games some sellers play

Game 1: **Churning** Replacing an existing non-term policy. A seller tells you that you can have more coverage for less premium with the new policy from some insurance company. You will pay the commission again and will end up with more premiums to pay and less actual account value over time. There is nothing new in insurance except for *lower* premiums for pure term insurance because we are living longer.

Game 2: **Two for one** Same as Game 1 except you keep the old policy and give up some of its value to buy a new one. Or the second one is paid by borrowing your account value from the first one. Eventually, the loan must be paid or you don't have the policy values left.

Game 3: **Signature form switch** Taking a loan on your existing policy requires you to sign. You signed a lot of forms. You don't remember signing the loan form? It was the fifth one in a row, I'll bet. Ask your Attorney General to help you cancel.

Game 4: **Vanishing premium** "... and you only have to pay the premiums for 8 years." That is what the agent promised. Of course, the agent cannot really see into the future and know that interest rates will remain high. If you get the statements in writing, the company will probably give you your money back. Get all seller promises in writing.

Game 5: **Retirement or savings plan** The seller promises you all your "deposits" will grow "tax-deferred" and far surpass your tiny bank CD or savings plan. You sign up and later find you have purchased another life insurance policy. The seller keeps 100% of your first year's payments. If you have the offer in writing, you can win a large settlement. See Chapter 4 to insure that you have enough to stop working when you want.

Game 6: **Nursing home coverage** Same as Game 5 but this time the seller uses the high cost of custodial care to scare you into buying life insurance. Some policies do allow you to take some of the death benefit if you become terminally ill. See our Insider's Guide to Long-term Care Insurance to save up to $2,000 per year.

Game 7: **College savings plan** Same as Game 5 but this time the seller uses the high cost of college to induce you to buy insurance with a savings or investment component. Yes, you can borrow from the policy to pay for college, but you can save for college on a tax-deferred basis at almost **half the price** using low-cost plans. See our Insider's Guide to Education Funding to save up to $20,000 in commission and fees over 18 years.

Game 8: **Pension maximization** This 'neat' idea does not work for everyone. The idea is good but the devil is in the details. A retiring worker has their spouse forgo the joint pension option so that they both can receive the larger single payout. The difference is used to buy a permanent policy. If the pensioner dies, the pension ends. The death benefit is supposed to provide the income the pension used to. Usually the payout difference is not enough to cover the premium needed to buy coverage. Double trouble is the premium must be paid even if the pension amount does not keep up with inflation. Triple trouble is the life insurance amount may not be enough for the spouse to live on. Can the spouse manage the investment of the death benefit?

Game 9: **Fake policy** Some reprehensible sellers have learned how to avoid the regulators because we have an ancient system of tracking agents. There are plenty of people who are not healthy and buy any policy out of fear. If the offer is legit, get it in writing. Call the state insurance regulator to verify the agent and offer.

Game 10: **Terms confuse**. Use this Glossary (http://www2.iii.org/glossary/) to confirm the offer's actual terms of coverage. Getting a second opinion does not cost anything and can save you big money.

EasySheet   Do you have enough life coverage?

Buy an amount of term so that your beneficiary can earn replacement income from 8% of the amount each year. Example: $500,000 policy benefit invested at 8% yields $40,000. $500,000 costs about $1 a day.

1. Family members depend on your income of $_____ (annual),

   Multiply by the number of years needed.*   ___ years

   Total amount needed $_____ .

2. Outstanding debts: Mortgage $_____ .
   (estimate)   Vehicles $_____ .
                               Credit cards $_____ .
                               Medical $_____ .
                               Other $_____ .

   Add total   + $_____ .

3. Income-producing assets:
                               Properties $_____ .
                               Securities $_____ .
                               Pensions $_____ .
                               Social security $_____ .

   Subtract total $ (_____)less

4. Other life insurance: Face amount $_____ .

   Subtract total $ (_____)less

   Amount Needed   (total the 4 steps) $_____

*Years needed: Your spouse may have a career and need only 2 years to adjust to your death. If your spouse does not have career prospects, use 4-6 years. Add 1-2 years for each young child. Spouse adjustment ____ + Child care years ____ = Total years ____ .

9

The Insider's Guide to Homeowner's Insurance: Beware false coverage

✓ Your policy may charge for rooms you don't have, or
✓ You may be paying for endorsements you don't need, or
✓ Your premium may be based on land value. It's not covered.
✓ Save up to $2,000 over 10 years.

What type do you need?

■ Your home and possessions can be insured for replacement prices or "depreciated" values. A 10-year-old recliner has a depreciated value of $20, for instance.
■ Higher deductibles reduce costs by up to 40%. Fewer claims keep your rates low.
■ Insure the actual house size and type for catastrophes. Declare new addition or pool!
■ Earthquakes, floods, and sewer back-up are **NOT covered** under standard policies.
■ Add another policy for flood and coastal storms.

The key question in homeowner's insurance is:

Are you willing to pay more every year to replace your home exactly as it is at the time of a total loss, even though a total loss is *very* rare?

A policy that exactly replicates your home, called "guaranteed replacement," costs more than "replacement—similar kind." If you have an older home, you may not be able to find a policy to rebuild your home exactly the way it is. This type of coverage is expensive because it pays up to and beyond the limit of the policy. Total destruction of your home is a very rare event because most of us pay fire departments to put out fires. Fewer than 2% of claims are for total loss. However, with the recent wildfires, more people are finding out that what they were sold—extended replacement—isn't a replacement policy". "Most people go to their insurance agent to buy coverage and figure they're fully covered," said J. Robert Hunter, the director for insurance at the Consumer Federation of America. "But often, they're not."

The next level of coverage is called "replacement cost" or "extended." This will cover the cost of rebuilding and replacing your home and possessions up to the limits of coverage. You must insure for at least 80% or 90% of the cost

> **Example of saving up to 22%:**
> Mary D. saw her premium fall 22% from $574 to $448 for a home valued at $250,000 with $1,000 deductible. Her home was misclassified as a multiple dwelling from a time when Mary owned rental property. She also dropped a Jewelry and Furs option since she has only family heirlooms that can't be replaced. Mary saves $126 over 10 years or about $2,500 in her Wealth Reserve.

of rebuilding of your home to have 100% replacement—"similar kind." Since the chance of total loss is remote, the policy will pay the full price to fix your kitchen if it is destroyed by fire, for instance. If the couch burns up, the insurer will supply a new one of comparable or similar value. (The insurer buys them below wholesale.) Many people pick this alternative. It covers most repairs but has a cap on the benefits. Most people need to add automatic inflation protection and building code improvements to their policy. Other options are listed below.

The next level of coverage is "actual cash value" reimbursement. With this policy, you are given only the amount that the insurer calculates is the value of your home and possessions, **as used**. What would your computer cost at a flee market, for instance? It may cost you a lot to rebuild and refurnish a room in your home if you had a major fire.

Remember, the mortgage is secured by your home and needs to be paid off if your home isn't there anymore. Land can't be insured so the price your new neighbor paid for their house (domania.com, zillow.com) is not a good indicator of the amount you would receive if there was a total loss. One of our members got a warning from their insurance company that the amount that the bank wanted on the policy to refinance the house was more than the insurer was willing to pay in case of loss. That means that the member is over-paying for the policy face amount and that if the house were a total loss today, the insurer's check may not be enough to pay off the mortgage.

Some people with older homes have this kind of policy. It is important to verify the actual cost to rebuild (Building-cost.net/CornersType.asp) your home. Would it make sense to rebuild if you can buy a similar home for the amount you receive from the insurance company, if you had no mortgage? Many people assume they will never have a total loss because it is very rare. If they have a partial loss, they will use their own funds from their savings for the deductible.

There is good reason to assume there will never be a total loss if you live in a town with a full-time fire department. The overall chance of having any fire is low, especially if your family does not smoke.

This Guide helps you take advantage of our insider's 'tricks of the trade.' You may not need some extra coverage riders, called 'endorsements.' These may include jewelry, furs, silverware, guns, workmen's compensation for the people you employ, sewer backup, identity theft, or watercraft. You can save up to 40% on your coverage by using the $2,500 deductible-level and discounts. You can re-direct your savings to your **Wealth Reserve**™. Your **Wealth Reserve**™ is your self-insurance fund to pay the first $2,500 of a claim if you ever have one.

There are about 8 claims filed per 100 house years (policies), according to the Insurance Information Institute (iii.org). The average homeowner files a claim about every 13 years. You will have an extra $3,900 in your **Wealth Reserve**™ by picking a higher deductible and investing the savings. If you don't have a loss, the $3,900 can be used to protect you against other risks.

You have another good reason to raise your deductible. You won't have small claims on your record. Some insurers have used the excuse of small claims to raise the premium or even drop your coverage. For instance, 25% of California homeowners who were dropped filed 1 or 2 non-water claims. 32% of those not renewed filed water damage claims. Overall, dog bite claims represent about 25% of all claims nationally. Some insurers have even put the record of a claim in the CLUE database even when there was *NO* claim paid. https://personalreports.lexisnexis.com/fact_act_disclosure.jsp Just asking the agent about a loss event has triggered the "zero-payout" loss (Realtytimes.com/rtcpages/20030512_clue.htm) entry. It is not fair, but it is their system.

WARNING: This Guide offers advice on how to **self-insure** yourself. This Guide shows you how to drop coverage you may not need. However, before you change your coverage, make certain that the alternative plan is in place. <u>Do not cancel your old policy</u> before you confirm your alternative policy is in force. Some insurers cancel the policy after they research your home's record. Start a **Wealth Reserve**™ today.

Our Insider said making two claims in a three-year period is more likely to flag your file. Many companies base their decisions on how long you've been with the company and the nature of the claims. For instance, many carriers keep a list of dog breeds most likely to attack. If you own that breed, it may be difficult to obtain or keep insurance. Damage from water may produce a flag. Carriers have begun to exclude mold coverage from their policies. You may be flagged if someone claims injury on your property.

Saving money on homeowner's insurance can also come from making sure that the insurer has accurate facts about your home. Some members found that when they move to a new home, some of the assumptions on the old home follow them. You may be paying more because the house size, type, proximity to shore or a hydrant, bad neighborhood, smoking status and use are wrong. For instance, one member moved from a multiple dwelling in Hudson County, New Jersey to a single residence in Morris County, New Jersey. The insurer changed the mortgage value and address but nothing else in the record. This member was overcharged for multiple dwelling and urban rates.

You may save money on the cost of coverage if you already have an excess liability or umbrella policy with your vehicle insurer. If you use the same insurer for all three, there is a discount. Make sure that the insurer knows that you don't have a man-eating dog, if you don't. You may save by having a good credit rating, an alarm, your age, nonsmokers, and the lack of jewels, furs, silverware, guns, and other things some folks like to steal. You may have to pay extra for decks, pools, business use, trees, and boats. The complete list of discounts is included on the **EasySheet** below.

Let's talk about the **special coverage** you may need on your policy. If you have antiques in your home, your policy will cover the current appraised value if you can prove it. That will require showing a proof of purchase, a new appraisal, a picture and other details which can be assembled using the instructions below. Today you can do this for everything in your home by creating a video.

Store the videotape and receipts with your relatives or attorney.

If you have specific items of great value, you can buy coverage just for them. Standard policies have limits. Your bank does not cover valuables in your safe-deposit box so ask your insurer about them. Most family heirlooms cannot be covered because they cannot be replaced. Perhaps a fire-rated safe in the basement would be best.

What is not covered?

Most of the things you would think are covered, are NOT:

Water damage: Floods, sewer backups, seepage, continuous leaks, and mold.
Disasters: Earthquakes, hurricanes, ice flows, war, nuclear, settling, and cracking.
Neglect: Damage or loss because you didn't do something. Normal wear and tear, animal or insect infiltration, smoke from industry, leaving property unprotected for over 30 days, lying about your dog or previous losses, and general maintenance. Insurance is NO substitute for home maintenance. Use this checklist to check. (http://www.wnins.com/products/pdf/hochecklist.pdf).

If you are in a flood zone, buy flood insurance http://www.floodsmart.gov/floodsmart/ since our taxes subsidize it. If you are near an earthquake fault, buy earthquake insurance. If your home is in the middle of a windy canyon or forest, buy windstorm insurance. If you want to live in a dangerous place, increase your self-insuring **Wealth Reserve**™.

Renters! Insurance is important to you because your landlord does not cover your possessions. Even if the landlord is at fault, you will not have the time or money to collect for your losses. According to a 2003 recent survey, 64 percent of respondents living in rental properties had no insurance. Landlords don't give tenants money to refurnish if there is a fire.

The most often **overlooked** coverage is excess or "umbrella" liability—lawsuit—coverage. This is a separate policy to protect your assets if you are sued. Since we have many more lawyers than any other country, you have a good chance of being sued. For instance, the policy pays the judgment and lawyer's fee when you are sued by the burglar who broke his leg jumping out your bedroom window after trying to steal your stuff. It happens. No kidding! The cost is less than $400 per $1 million. Use our Insider's Guide to "Lawsuit" Insurance.

What to avoid

- ✓ Avoid using the closing lawyer's agent. Shop around! Discounts can save you $2,500.
- ✓ Paying for land, floor space, rooms, luxury goods and zoning you don't have.

If you are in the process of buying a home, avoid using the real estate agency or bank lawyer as a referral source for insurance. You can save up to 40% on the cost of insurance by shopping the customer-focused carriers listed below. Ask your vehicle insurer for a discount. Rates vary by 50% and can save you $2,500 over 10 years.

> **. . . they want good value, not 'good hands'.**

Don't assume that your home is classified correctly for risks. Carriers do not always visit a home before insuring it. They may use the zip code of the property to classify it. If your home is different from those around you, you should provide the real estate agency description of the property. Carriers have different rate-tiers and discount programs. The only way to know if you are overpaying for insurance is to compare the prices of three insurers. Use the **EasySheet** below.

Don't lie about the condition of the property. The carriers search a national database of properties, called "CLUE." If there was a claim in the past, it is probably already known to the underwriter. The database makes it difficult for some people to obtain homeowner's cover on the homes they just bought (Realtytimes.com/rtnews/rtcpages/20030512_clue.htm). Check to make sure your home's "rap" sheet is clean at lexisnexis.com/fact_act_claims_bundle/landing.jsp. You can ask the seller to provide the report before you purchase a home. By the way, you can also check on contractors and other vital records there.

How much coverage do you need?

Buy just enough to protect your home and assets. If you own property where land values are high, the land might be worth more than the house. Old homes around you might be selling for $500,000, but the most the insurance company will have to pay to rebuild is $250,000. You don't need $1/2 million in coverage, you only need $250,000. The difference is hundreds of premium dollars each year.

    Insure against the most likely losses. A kitchen fire will usually be stopped before it takes your whole house. A comprehensive HO-3 policy with replacement cost coverage of 100% of the cost of rebuilding is your best value. If your home cost $200,000 to rebuild, a policy for $200,000 would cover most losses in full (minus the deductible).

    A higher deductible policy costs less. You can profit from the investment of part of the premium instead of your insurer. If you maintain your property, you will have fewer claims. This will keep your premium from being raised. You lower the risk of being dropped due to frequent small claims, as some homeowner's discovered in California.
(Consumersunion.org/pub/core_financial_services/000218.html)

    If your home is damaged or possessions stolen worldwide, your carrier will be the primary payer. Home accidents are not usually "total" losses. Insuring older homes for "guaranteed replacement cost" is expensive. Compare "replacement cost-similar."

- Your valuables are protected to a limit. Your heirlooms can't be replaced but hobbies and collections can be insured. See our **EasySheet** below. Get the coverage in writing.
- Without proper documentation of possessions and proof of loss to show the carrier, full coverage may yield an unfair settlement. A videotape and receipts are the best 'proof.' Video your garage, basement and yard contents too. Complete the List below. Locks must show "forced entry" for a theft claim. A public adjuster or insurance attorney can help with big claims.
- If you are sued, the policy will defend you and pay the judgment to a limit. You will not have to sell your home or business if you add an "Umbrella" personal liability policy. You can obtain $1,000,000 coverage for less than $400 from your auto carrier. See **The Insider's Guide to "Lawsuit" Insurance.**

- The wording of insurance policies is confusing and unclear. Ask "what would happen if" questions about a hypothetical accident—a fire in your kitchen, for instance. Compare how the carriers would reimburse you. Repairs should include local code upgrades.

Best value for your needs

- ✓ "Direct writers" focus on you, not on their agents.
- ✓ 100% of the rebuilding cost with an inflation endorsement.
- ✓ Raise the deductible to $2500 or more and save up to 40%.
- ✓ Ask for each discount separately to save up to 30%. See our **EasySheet** below.

The best value is the policy that fits your lifestyle needs. "Direct writer" carriers are more focused on your needs than on their salespeople. The insurer may be organized as a mutual company, like Amica, paying a dividend (return of premium). Since they rely on word of mouth for new sales, they take pride in settling claims quickly. You deal directly with the insurer. Agents don't decide your claim settlement so shop for coverage. The insurer with the absolute lowest price will change over time because insurers change marketing and investment strategies.

Most insurance agents purchase a comprehensive (HO-3) homeowner's policy for "replacement-similar kind" with a high deductible for their own home. That policy takes care of 99% of the claims and saves them 20-40% a year. They understand that they need to maintain the property to prevent it from deteriorating to a loss. You can prevent losses and save money too. By investing that 40% savings each year, your self-insuring **Wealth Reserve**™ will cover the deductible for a claim, if necessary. Since claims are infrequent, your **Wealth Reserve**™ can grow each year.

You can learn how to prevent losses. For instance, agents use a checklist of the common problems that lead to losses. Simple things like cleaning your dryer's lint exhaust, replacing washer hoses, and locating your inside water cutoff valve in case of flooding can provide you with peace of mind. One member installed a $5 battery-powered alarm on the basement floor to warn of any water leaks immediately. Another member has a wet/dry vacuum next to the water heater in case of leaks. By learning the 'tricks of the trade' you can save money and feel confident.

Most people need the inflation protection endorsement. This keeps your coverage current with the cost of rebuilding. Inform the insurer of any significant change to your property. A pool increases the chance of a suit which can take all your assets. If you have not informed the insurer, you might not have enough policy protection. An umbrella policy that covers your assets is a necessity today. It pay the lawyer and judgment, if needed.

How and where to buy

- Shop for the best price. Contact Geico.com (800-841-2964), Electricinsurance.com (800-342-5342), Amica.com (800-242-6422), 21st.quoteweb/ (877-834-7532), NetQuote.com and Homesite.com (800-947-0713).
- For veterans, call USAA.com (800-365-8722) and Afi.org (800-255-6792).
- New Jersey company employees, New Jersey Manufacturers (njm.com/ 800-232-6600).
- Your Credit union (CreditUnion.coop), union or association, or vehicle insurer.
- National Flood Insurance information: floodsmart.gov (888 379-9531).

It can take only 30 minutes on the phone or Internet to obtain quality coverage for less. The cost of homeowner's for the same property can vary widely. Compare at least three providers using the **EasySheet** below.

Don't drop your old policy until the new one is in force for 30 days!

This may include an inspection. Most people remain with their carrier for many years, so the savings you find will accumulate over time. Some members have saved $2,500 in 10 years. You have to ask for each discount to get them though.

Since title insurance covers a very small risk of improper ownership, only **about 5 cents of every dollar collected in premiums is paid out in claims!** One in three properties has some complication or defect with its title that needs to be fixed before the final sale. It covers boundary issues, which may go to court. Obtain quotes from insurers: homeclosing101.org/shopping.cfm

If your state provides comparison data like New Jersey (State.nj.us/dobi/homeown.htm) does, you can see that the same HO-3 policy can cost between $421 and $1,788. Mutual companies, like Amica, may return a part of your premium each year. Find your state at Naic.org/state_web_map.htm.

Avoid using the agent recommended by the real estate agency or the mortgage bank if you are buying your first home. The insurer usually pays a fee for this referral. If your friends and family love their agent, compare their quotes with "direct writers." You want the best price for a standard policy in most cases because most homeowner's contracts are very similar. The exception is Texas, which has a different set of basic forms. Policy HO-B and C are the most comprehensive.

It is impossible to know in advance how you will be treated if you have a claim. Amica and USAA have won awards for the service they provide. Customers do not switch without good reason. The largest companies, State Farm and Allstate, have the largest number of complaints, which makes sense since they have more claims (consumeraffairs.com/). If you have an idea of what to expect from your insurer, you might be able to handle a claim better. On the other hand, hiring a public adjuster (napia.com) might help convince the insurer you deserve a "*fair-er*" settlement.

The critical policy elements

1. Select a company with high financial strength "A" rating.
2. Delete endorsements/riders you don't use—firearms, gems, furs, silverware, workman's comp.
3. Amica and USAA have the highest customer loyalty scores.
4. Confirm you have been placed in the best risk classification possible.
5. Confirm you have all possible discounts and correct building-type tier.

Insuring your special needs

- ✓ Foremost.com (888-814-8832) insures recreation homes.
- ✓ Your union or association may offer coverage with discounts.
- ✓ Your vehicle carrier or a specialist may offer coverage.
- ✓ SeniorResource.com has information about remodeling your home to meet your needs.
- ✓ Boat coverage at Progressive.com (800-288-6776).

Seek a carrier that specializes in your special needs. Recreation homes require special provisions. For instance, most policies do not cover homes that are vacant for over 30 days. Custom-built homes require special coverage to rebuild the features. Unusual and expensive homes and contents can be covered completely for a price. However, most financially independent people weigh the full premium payments against the unlikely event of a loss.

Your profession or hobby-business use of your home may add risks that a basic policy is not designed for. Check with your insurer if you have business-related property with you outside of work. For instance, a member lost a very fine camera while shooting a wedding as a hobby-small business. The camera was not covered. Also if someone at the wedding was hurt through the negligence or accident of the member, this liability is not covered. The member also found that a power outage caused by the failure of the local utility to fix a damaged transformer was not a covered cause of the loss of computer equipment and data. Some members discovered that the cost of their policy went down when they made the rooms in their homes more accessible.

How carriers decide to insure you

- ✓ Your home's repair history, size, rooms, construction, age, zip code, and use.
- ✓ Carriers use your age, lifestyle, claims and credit records.
- ✓ Average cost of repairs in your area, crime records and sprinkler equipment.
- ✓ Choice of deductible: Fewer large claims are preferred to many small claims.
- ✓ Timing: Carriers' marketing and investment strategies change.

What to do if they did not renew

Clearly, they made a mistake! The whole purpose of insurance is that when you have a loss, everyone pays a penny to make you whole. Unfortunately, most insurers are now owned by institutional shareholders who want steadily increasing returns and who are willing to pay a CEO $ millions in salary/bonus/severance to make it so, even if they can't. ***It is not fair***, but it is the system we have.

We think customer-focused carriers like Amica and GEICO and USAA want to keep good customers—not drop you when you happen to be a burglary victim twice. On the other hand, insurers must battle the ever-growing industry of insurance fraud.

First. Find out the reason for being dropped. If you were robbed, protect yourself with a *faux* sign (ebay.com has fake "security sign"), deadbolts, or an alarm. You will probably receive a discount to offset the cost. Give yourself enough time to find new coverage before the expiration date. **Don't cancel your old policy before you have your new one in force for over 60 days**.

Second. Shop for a new policy. In most cases, one bad patch of luck does not disqualify you. Some insurers are looking for new customers while others are not. In 2008-2009, some of the big public companies stopped writing new insurance because they lost money in the stock market. Policies are liabilities to them so they had to match their reduced asset size to keep their financial ratings. They did not have enough reserves to cover more people.

Third. Most states have programs for "under-served" areas or "FAIR plan" for those who can't get insurance. Texans went through extraordinarily difficult times recently because insurers left. In California, costs are so high that moving to a safer city might be the only choice for some families. Find yours Naic.org/state_web_map.htm.

Fourth. When you find a new policy, don't cancel the old one until the new one is in force at least two month. Some companies underwrite AFTER they take your money.

EasySheet Find the best coverage and discounts

	Company A	Company B	Company C
Name			

Premium: _Annual _Semi _Quarter

	Company A	Company B	Company C
Dwelling and extension (replacement-similar)	$	$	$
Personal property damage or loss	$	$	$
Loss of Use (motel bill)	$	$	$
Personal liability	$	$	$
Property damage of others	$	$	$
Medical payments to others	$	$	$
Inflation increases 3%, 5%	?$	$	$
Coverage deductibles $1,000 (24% off) $2,500 (40% off)	$	$	$
Grand Total	$	$	$

Ask for discounts:

	Company A	Company B	Company C
New home (under 7 years)	[]	[]	[]
Annual payment discount	[]	[]	[]
Multi-home (vacation)	[]	[]	[]
Multi-policy (car, umbrella)	[]	[]	[]
Non-smoking (1/3 fires caused by smokers)	[]	[]	[]
Good credit risk	[]	[]	[]
Low claim rate-no dog, boat or precious gems	[]	[]	[]
Smoke detector	[]	[]	[]
Burglar alarm/central service	[]	[]	[]
Sprinkler system	[]	[]	[]
Retired and over 55 years	[]	[]	[]
At home family member	[]	[]	[]
Longevity with carrier 6+ years	[]	[]	[]
Hydrant/firehouse location	[]	[]	[]
Affinity group membership	[]	[]	[]
Other _____	[]	[]	[]

Umbrella personal liability coverage
	Company A	Company B	Company C
$1,000,000 Protection	$	$	$

If you have a claim, these tips from our Insider attorney will help you win.

- Get organized. Document your claim. Communicate often by email, letter and take notes of conversations. Keep every note about how and when repairs were done. Perhaps your insurance provider is insisting that you weren't covered for this particular kind of damage. Ask your provider to show you exactly where in your policy it states this type of loss/damage was not covered. For instance, some policies will not cover a fire caused by an auxiliary heating system.

- Be precise and accurate in the Proof of Loss statement. If you are unsure how to fill out a claim form, ask the staff of the **National Insurance Consumer Helpline**, 800-942-4242. Use photos extensively. Don't exaggerate or misrepresent your claim. Fraud is a big concern for insurers. Meet with adjuster at loss site.

- If you've gone over the fine print and dispute your insurance company's decision, there are several steps you can take. Ask your insurer to put the reason for the denial in writing. Call the senior claims manage" and provide reasons for your view. Ask to speak to the company ombudsman. Finally, send a letter summarizing the dispute to the President of the company. Let the top person know you are going to the regulators next.

- Hire experts: If the fire origin is disputed, retain an expert at an early stage, before crucial evidence is destroyed. An experienced insurance lawyer will know the appropriate expert to hire. Half of all Katrina victims had no flood insurance so they lost all. Those that had it are glad they kept paying the $350 per year. Most have renewed since new rates aren't in yet.

- Many states offer help through an Insurance **Ombudsman or mediator**. Check your state Naic.org/state_web_map.htm. Claim dispute assistance is also available at the National Insurance Consumer Help line, 800-942-4242. Some insurers use a two-step process (depreciation loss) to wear you out.

- Be persistent. Decide up-front that you will become the 'squeaky wheel.' An insurance company does not like to pay claims. Sometimes only repeated requests will get action. Using public adjuster (Napia.com) can help. http://www.getclaimhelp.com/public-adjuster/10-worst-

insurance-companies-deny-claims-raise-premiums.html
- The final step is hiring a lawyer which will cost you. Often the most important factor in obtaining a fair settlement is to convince the carrier that you are willing to go to trial. Insurers know that a jury is your friend not theirs. Sometimes a TV news show will help you.

List Your Most Valuable Possessions
Store this list or video tape with a relative or advisor

Item description   Cost

Your obligations if you have a loss

1. Give prompt notice of a loss to the carrier or agent.
2. Notify police of a theft. Keep records.
3. Make temporary repairs to protect property from further damage.
4. Cooperate in the investigation and settlement.
5. Prepare an inventory of damaged property with receipts and documents.
6. Answer questions about the damaged property and loss proofs.
7. Provide a sworn proof of loss to the insurer within 60 days of request, including loss details, liens, other policies, title, and repair estimates.
8. You can't sue unless all conditions are met and not later than 1 year.
9. Insurer may replace or repair any part of the damaged property or take all or any of the property at the value stated in the policy after you accept the settlement.
10. Loss payment will be made in 60 days of the receipt of loss if you agree to the loss or there is a final judgment or appraisal is filed.
11. You cannot abandon property to the insurer. Recovered property may be returned to you with adjustment made to the loss payment.
12. You may loose coverage for important concealment or misrepresentation, non-payment of premium, change in risks, with 30 days notice.
13. You can't pursue a cause of loss on your own.
14. New additions or increases in the value of your property.

What is not covered without rider or extra policy

✗ A repair done in compliance with today's building codes.
✗ Earth movement from earthquakes, landslides, mud flows or earth sinking.
✗ Water damage from floods, sewers, seepage below ground, hurricane limit.
✗ Power failure, neglect after a loss, war, nuclear, or intentional losses.
✗ Failure to act or decide and faulty, inadequate or defective repairs or maintenance.
✗ Wear and tear, defects, breakdowns, rust, mold, rot, contamination, smog, settling, cracking, shrinkage, damage from animals (pets), or weather conditions.
✗ Trees, shrubs and other plants lost in windstorm.
✗ Deductibles apply for each loss each time it happens; **NOT** once a year.
✗ Limits may apply for money, securities, deeds, IOUs, watercraft, trailers, collections, firearms, silverware, computers, rugs, tapestry, furs, jewelry, and music players.
✗ Animals, vehicles, tapes or tape players or device in vehicles, aircraft, boarders, books of account, records, drawings, rental apartment property.
✗ Workman's compensation liability of temporary worker.
✗ Liability due to willful and malicious acts or running a business or service.
✗ Heating oil tank in ground.
✗ Damage from mold and mildew. Some hurricane wind damage.

Your Action Plan

This week:
Goal

_____
_____

This month:
Goal

_____
_____
_____

This year:
Goals

_____
_____
_____
_____
_____
_____
_____
_____
_____

10

The Insider's Guide to Health Insurance: Affordable health insurance

Yes, you can find it!

1. Your employer does not provide it, or
2. You are self-employed, or
3. You want to supplement the gaps in your current policy.
4. Save $5,000 over 10 years with the right plan.

Pick the right plan for your needs

- ✓ HMO, if your primary family doctor accepts HMO and your family needs are routine.
- ✓ PPO, if your favorite doctor is a Preferred Provider and your needs are infrequent.
- ✓ Will an HMO cover your special situation, close to home, offer optional benefits?
- ✓ The self-employed and healthy benefit from a Health Savings Account (HSA).

This Guide helps you find affordable medical care for your needs. The goal is to find a comprehensive medical plan that *your* doctors accept at a reasonable cost. If your employer subsidizes care, there are usually plan choices to make. If you are on your own, affordable medical care is possible when you use a self-insurance plan.

Ask your family doctor or the doctor you see the most if they accept the plan you are considering. For most people, this is the most important question to answer.

> **Example of saving up to 25%**: A health plan for Mr. D's family required an hour on Golden Rule to complete an application for three for a PPO policy. The cost is $194.40 per month, 25% less than a quote from local agent: $1,000 deductible, 80/20% with a $10,000 stop-loss limit, $3,000,000 for life. The carrier rated "A" by A.M.Best.

The person in charge of billing in the doctor's office can help you learn which plans would cover all of your ordinary visits.

They can help you determine if the reimbursement rate is acceptable to the doctor without you having to pay more.

HMO and EPO plans that include most of your family's routine visits might be the best value. HMO medical care has been satisfactory for many families despite the bad press. HMO patients who get to see their regular doctors at little cost are pleased with their HMO plans, according to patient surveys. If you need child medical care, the HMO plan may be the best value if it covers all your routine visits and big expenses like surgery. If you have few medical needs, most HMOs will cover all your care due to an accident or long illness.

HMO and EPO plans may not have a specialist in your area. Consider your past medical needs before you sign up. If someone in your family has an emergency, where will they be taken? Check to see which hospital would be used for routine surgery, like having your child's tonsils removed. Where would you be sent for physical therapy after an accident? HMO's may limit services or engage institutions far away for such medical help. HMO's can decide not to save your life. However, if they make a bad decision (1 chance in 83,720), they can't be sued according to the US Supreme Court.

PPO plans work well for those who see specialists on a regular basis or want to pick their own doctors. Depending on the plan, your favorite doctors may be covered to 70% or 80% of the fee. If you have used the same doctor for years, you may be able to negotiate a lower out-of-pocket fee. The person responsible for reimbursements in the doctor's office can help you determine how to make this arrangement. These plans can be cost-effective if you have a large deductible policy. You insure against the large unforeseen expenses while paying for your known medical needs yourself.

Self-employment medical care may be cheaper using a <u>Health Savings Account</u> (<u>irs.gov/publications/p969/ar02.html#en_US_2010_publink1000204020</u>). You can use pre-tax dollars to pay for medical needs in combination with a high deductible catastrophic policy. This can provide a combination of coverage. You pay for small expenses from an account that grows tax-deferred. Clinics in medical schools, drug stores or health fairs are cheaper. Pick the <u>best</u> and specialty <u>hospitals</u> <u>healthgrades.com/</u>. You can negotiate charges based on

costs. cms.hhs.gov/HealthCareConInit/02_Hospital.asp
Seek medical advice. You have full coverage for unforeseen large medical bills. You insure yourself for part of your medical needs. This method is part of the self-directed medical care trend.

Your small business has access to a group rate plan. Your health insurance premiums are deductible business expenses. Your association or chamber of commerce may provide a group rate you can use. There are now more opportunities for group rates than before, including college alumni and AAA. Only 5% of eligible employees have enrolled in employer HSA plans. Your state insurance department may have information about how to obtain state (PA, MA, HI, IL, ME) coverage, or group coverage or qualify for small business rates. Check your state at NAIC.org.

If you are on your own, affordable medical care is possible when you employ a form of self-insurance coverage. If you are in good health, you can buy a comprehensive policy that covers your catastrophic comprehensive medical care needs. This kind of policy pays for most hospital and doctor bills if you have an accident or sickness that requires a long stay or surgery. In return for a reasonable premium, you pay for ordinary doctor visits and prescriptions. Benefits usually include paying all of your bills beyond your limit of responsibility, usually $1,000 to $10,000. Premiums are as low as $30 a month.

This maximum medical outlay can be anticipated by building a Health Savings Account or a **Wealth Reserve**™. You can accumulate your **Wealth Reserve**™ using the money you saved from our Insider Guides. Your savings can amount to $3,000 per year. Our advice is to use the savings to buy assets that "grow by themselves." Over time, your Self-Insurance **Wealth Reserve**™ can provide funding for most of your spending needs, including medical care. It would cover your medical expenses up to the deductible and stop-loss limit of your policy.

The recommendations in this Guide assume that you will fund or have funded your **Wealth Reserve**™. Your **Wealth Reserve**™ helps you become financially independent because you are not making *others* rich. You use your income to buy "assets that grow by themselves."

You can buy a comprehensive individual health policy that covers your catastrophic medical care needs directly from some insurance companies. If you are in good health, you can complete the application in about 15 minutes and obtain a quote. These companies, called "direct writers," include GoldenRule.com and Celtic-net.com. They offer you comprehensive coverage in most parts of the country. Some require a membership fee in order to qualify for their rates.

The Health Savings Account HD-HSA allows you to pay for qualified medical expenses with pre-tax dollars (income-tax free!). This is like your **Wealth Reserve**™ but separate. You can pay for plan deductibles, co-pays, coinsurance, drugs, dental, vision, psychiatric, long-term care, and transportation to care. You can't use an H.S.A. for the actual premiums unless you are unemployed. You can contribute up to the plan's annual deductible. You access the account with special checks or debit cards. At the end of the year, you can deduct the amount paid into the account like you would an IRA.

You can obtain the account when you apply for the H.S.A.-qualified health insurance plan. The qualified plans have a name or symbol to designate those that have higher deductibles and thus need a special source of funding. You are paying something for your own care and can determine to some degree what your medical care costs are. Unfortunately, some H.S.A.-vendors charge a fee for their services. Compare the fee to other providers before you sign up. See hsabank.com/HSABank/Accountholders.aspx for example..

WARNING: This Guide offers advice on how to self-fund your purchases. This Guide shows you how to save by paying cash from your **Wealth Reserve**™ for things in your spending plan. Do not use money designated for your long-term goals (401k, college or IRA funds) to pay for short-term needs. Start your **Wealth Reserve**™ NOW!

If you are age 65 or over, your choice is Medicare and a Medigap supplement policy. You can find information on these policies at Medicare.gov. With each policy A-J, you can buy additional benefits. However, if you have a **Wealth Reserve**™ established, you may save by purchasing only the Basic "A" services.

Compare drug effectiveness at OregonRX.org, CRbestbuydrugs.org, and Aarp.org before buying your drug plan at Medicare.gov. Check pparx.org for free care.

What to avoid

- ✓ Specific ailment, amount or event. Buy a comprehensive policy with a higher deductible.
- ✓ Non-renewable or cancelable. Buy only noncancelable or guaranteed renewable.
- ✓ Low ($250,000) maximum, high stop-loss, deductible per person.
- ✓ Poorly run plans: check US News survey: usnews.com/directories/health-plans/index_html

The first objective of medical coverage is to have a plan that covers expenses that **could** take all your assets. You want the policy to cover *all* expenses for the big things—surgery or cancer treatment—to an unlimited lifetime max. Buy for a **catastrophic** event. Most bankruptcies are caused by unpaid medical expenses.

The second objective is to buy a comprehensive policy so that all the services associated with a catastrophic event are covered: Doctors, surgeons, techs, nursing, treatment, x-rays, oxygen, bandages, hospital room and meals, medicines, tests, etc, etc. Compare maximum out-of-pocket costs and maximum limit. Pick $3,000 coinsurance cap or stop-loss limit and unlimited lifetime maximum expenses.

The third objective is to cover large expenses that are more likely; avoiding plans that insure less-likely situations. You are more likely to be injured in a car crash than to develop cancer if you are under 65 years old, for instance. A family without kids can absorb doctor visits but not an emergency appendectomy.

Plans that pay a fixed amount per illness or procedure should be avoided. If you have a hospital indemnity plan that pays for $500 a day, who will pay for the rest of the bill? Medical costs rise quickly and a fixed amount will be exceeded within minutes of admission. Without a comprehensive policy, you will be billed the retail price, not what insurers pay. Plans that cover only one ailment or event like cancer insurance should be avoided. These are very popular in Canada because national health care covers all. Insurers have nothing else to sell. People fear cancer but insurance won't prevent it. Most standard policies cover all ailments, so there is no need to pay for a separate (e.g. cancer) policy.

Plans that offer supplemental benefits should be avoided

because you are paying for benefits you would already have in a comprehensive policy. If there are specific areas of benefits that you believe are thin in your current coverage, ask the seller or insurer about adding a rider to your existing policy. Avoid policies that use "<u>post-claim underwriting</u>." It is used to cancel coverage after you file a claim.

Sellers of accident and medical insurance are not in a good position to offer unbiased advice about what you need. The seller is paid for sales based upon the total premium. If you are offered options, like ambulance coverage or accidental death and dismemberment coverage, check your existing policy. You will find that accidents are covered in a comprehensive policy. Our other Guides can help you insure your life and disability payments separately for less. Health insurers do not usually offer the best value for life and disability protection.

Make policy lapse impossible

Check that your comprehensive insurance policy is noncancelable or guaranteed renewable. Confirm with the insurer that you will not be dropped if you pay your premium. Establish an automatic deduction from your bank account or credit card to make sure a lapse is not possible. Your premium can be increased if everyone in your class of coverage is increased. You should expect increases. Buy a policy with a higher deductible so that increases are less likely. Use the savings to build your **Wealth Reserve**™.

Confirm that your comprehensive policy provides you with no lifetime maximum or at least $3 million. Find a plan with a family deductible. If your spouse has high expenses one year, you don't want to spend the amount again for yourself or others. Make sure that the coverage has a stop-loss low enough for you to handle in a year. Your Health Savings Account or **Wealth Reserve**™ can be built up to cover this amount using automatic monthly investments. With this method, you are using your income to buy "assets that grow by themselves" instead of giving the money to the insurer. You are paying lower premiums so that the insurer pays for truly catastrophic claims, like a car accident or heart attack.

Know your obligations and rights according to the contract. For instance, some plans make you call your primary doctor if you have to go to the emergency room over the weekend. If you don't call, **you are not covered** or reimbursed and may end up with a dispute between the hospital and the insurer. Other plans have different addresses for different kinds of claims—doctor, hospital, drug, or behavioral. Other plans change participating doctors and clinics almost daily. If your doctor wants blood done, the lab you went to last week may not be the place under contract this week. Call first. Always obtain a referral slip even if you've been to the same doctor before. Each specialist follow-up visit may require a new one from your primary doctor.

Check your reimbursement checks and statements. One member found that even though their child was covered, the insurance firm's clerks kept denying coverage because the insurer's computer was NOT programmed for her age group. The member had to call each time it occurred over a five-year period. Remember, most insurers are now using clerks in other countries to process your medical claims. U.S. privacy and fraud laws do not cover how your records are used outside the U.S. Check each benefit statement and reimbursement. Ask your doctor to restrict data sharing.

Appeal every claim denial

Contest any claim that is denied. Former health company employees have testified that some companies always deny claims the first time they are submitted. The statistics show you have a good chance to win the appeal if you follow the official procedures to appeal the denial. The 'squeaky wheel' usually finds a way to get fixed. Use this formal appeal letter.

The key to obtaining the maximum benefit from your insurance policy is to keep accurate records. Most plans have an appeals procedure. You must file your appeal within **certain limits** or you will lose your right to appeal. Make sure you understand and carefully follow the appeals process spelled out in your insurance plan booklet. If they claim the procedure is "investigational" or "experimental" and therefore not covered, contact an advocacy group in that field, like the Childhood Cancer Ombudsman Program. Your doctor may be able to provide you with journal articles and/or letters from other doctors that support the treatment.

Ask PatientAdvocate.org Foundation (800.532.5274). Check cms.hhs.gov/HealthCareConInit/02_Hospital.asp#TopOfPage for cost data.

Advocacy groups help families maximize benefits or resolve disputes. Call your elected representative to the US Congress also. All Senators and members of the House of Representatives have staff that help constituents with problems. Some members have asked the local paper to highlight a human interest story. Finally, take your claim to small claims court, or hire an attorney skilled in insurance matters to sue the insurance company. Above all, don't be afraid to ask questions, and be persistent!

Buy comprehensive coverage

The most important aspect to finding cost-effective health care is to match the plan to your lifestyle. A review of your coverage can save money now and slow further premium increases.

If you have just left an employer that provided coverage, you have the right to continue the policy but at full cost. Members who priced this alternative were shocked at the price. You can buy a short-term policy that provides some protection temporarily. Perhaps you will find a new employer, start your own business or become covered under your spouse's policy. One member found a new plan they could afford and asked their doctor to join so they could continue with the doctor. The doctor agreed.

A recent alternative for coverage is to buy a catastrophic policy for your family and use the Health Savings Account to pay for the higher deductibles. You don't lose the tax-advantages dollars in your H.S.A. if you don't use them. You may save $5,000 over 10 years using this method. You can only pay medical expenses—not premiums—from this account however.

✔ If your family members require frequent routine or child preventive care, an HMO or EPO will be the most cost effective. If you are single with few needs, a high deductible policy lets you save money while covering huge bills. Depending on your income, the PPO allowance for choices may be the best compromise for older family members. Determine needs from past year medical necessities. Anticipate major expenses. Ask the reimbursement person in your family doctor's office which plan is best for you. Ask your employer about all the alternatives.

✔ Pick a comprehensive major medical standard policy with highest family deductible you can afford. Check exclusions, pre-existing and pretreatment rules. Start a **Wealth Reserve**™ to cover deductibles.

✔ Choose optional coverages with care—premiums and deductibles cost more than wise out-of-pocket expense choice. For example, an annual dental checkup costs less than $20-per-month dental insurance policy costs. Use the **EasySheet** below to compare.

✔ If you have coverage with gaps from your current employer, check for additional coverage from your union or association. See You Have Rights below.

✔ The wording of an insurance policy is confusing and unclear. Ask what would happen with typical claims for immunizations, cold, surgery, pregnancy or an emergency. More information at MedLincPlus.org WebMD.com and CRBestBuyDrugs.org.

Best value

✓ HMO, EPO or PPO from a buying group or not-for-profit association. Glossary webmd.com/
✓ Renewal guaranteed, with "pre-existing" condition accepted and illnesses covered.
✓ HSA for pre-tax contributions and tax benefits.
✓ Family deductible, few exclusions, low stop-loss limit, high max, 20% co-pay.
✓ Checkout doctors before use. healthgrades.com, Webmd.com, HealthCentral.com, cdc.gov, and MayoClinic.com name specialists. Ask your family doctor. CastleConnolly.com provides lists of top docs. Google your doctor's name and practice.
✓ Check hospital scores at HHS.gov and qualitycheck.org and leapfroggroup.org/cp and hospitals.nyhealth.gov/ (New York), phc4.org (Pennsylvania) http://www.nahdo.org/map (other states).

The best value is a comprehensive plan that you can afford that includes your family doctor. Most people see their family doctor frequently. A plan that charges $20 each time you visit may be cheaper than a plan that pays more of the larger bill. For instance, a policy with $20 co-pay, 80/20% benefit with a $10,000 stop-loss limit is better than one with $0 co-pay, 70/30% with no stop-loss. You will pay more for ordinary visits but you will pay less if you have an accident or surgery is required. With one you know what you will pay. With the other, there is no limit.

You need a policy that can't be cancelled. Remember, it is the unforeseen accident or illness that usually wipes people out. Find a policy that you can afford now. If you are healthy, skip the bells and whistles—dental, vision, drug, and other add-ons. Use a Health Savings Account or your own **Wealth Reserve**™ for these and deductibles.

If you have a health condition, find a plan that covers your usual medical services. Ask about a preexisting condition. A pre-existing condition will be covered without a waiting period when you join a new group plan if you have been insured the previous 12 months. This means that if you remain insured for 12 months or more, you will be able to go from one job to another, and your pre-existing condition will be covered—without additional waiting periods—even if you have a chronic illness.

If you have a pre-existing condition and have not been insured the previous 12 months before joining a new plan, the longest you will have to wait before you are covered for that condition is 12 months. Check coverage for pregnancy and disabling illnesses. Some insurers cut back benefits in this area. Agents cannot make the insurer comply with their promises.

Check generic equivalent drugs at FDA.gov. Some insurers have negotiated prices on some name-brand drugs that are LESS than generics. AMBest.com

Check if your doctors are part of your plan. One member asked his doctor to join his employer's plan. She did. Check the doctors you are referred out to. Over 20,000 doctors have been disciplined in the last decade. Most are still in the business. Doctors' records are protected by the state. A national registry of bad docs is kept by Congress but we do not have access. However, you can find some information at Citizen.org, DocBoard.org, Abms.org and knowx.com. Some states don't post disciplinary information. In some states, you may be able to get the information by calling the medical board. (See fsmb.org/directory_smb.html) A study on Doctors Sanctioned for Sex Offenses Still Practicing was last done in 2000! It concludes:

Most doctors who were disciplined for the five most serious offenses were not required to stop practicing, even temporarily. (mercola.com/2000/aug/20/dangerous_doctors.htm)

You can look up some doctors and providers at Vitals.com and healthgrades.com. Other patients have given their opinions. There may be information listed if the doctor was sanctioned. However, you must call the board to see why. If there is a discrepancy between reports and the Abms.org data, ask your doctor for clarification. If the board has negative information, consider another doctor. The boards don't act without serious concerns. On the other hand, if you see a couple of $30,000 pay outs on the record, the doctor's insurer probably just settled without fault being found. Move on if there are 6 or more pay outs. Doctors are usually NOT forced to stop "practicing" on us. More people die from medical errors than car accidents (43,458), breast cancer (42,297), or AIDS (16,516). Check hospitals too.

How and where to buy

✓ Compare QuickQuote.com (800-867-2404), and eHealthInsurance.com (800-977-8860), healthmarkets.com/
✓ Direct Golden Rule.com, Celtic-net.com, Blue Cross Blue Shield bcbs.com, Aetna.com, UnitedHealthCare.com, HealthyNewYork (ins.state.ny.us/website2/hny/english/hny.htm), MA mahealthconnector.org
✓ Contact your school, association, fraternal, religious group, or your state at NAIC.org.
✓ If you have a small business, check for a group policy.
✓ If you just left your job or college, you may qualify for your old benefits under COBRA dol.gov or 2011 health law.

You can find a low-cost plan in about 15 minutes online. Some Internet sites provide rates, some have agents contact you. If you know what you want and can afford, shopping can help lower the price. Use the **EasySheet** below to compare rates and benefits. Consolidators, like QuickQuote, do not quote from all the insurers available in your state. Some states, like NJ, provide a list the insurers licensed in the state. Check your state at NAIC.org. Medical plan fraud (for example State.nj.us/dobi/ is rampant so check licenses before signing.

Obtain a quote from any organizations you belong to. Group rates are usually better than individual policies. Some policies sold by the direct writers, like Celtic and Golden Rule, are really group policies that require you to join a group of people buying insurance. Compare rates closely. Some Blue Cross plans may fit your lifestyle.

Your small business may obtain group rates and the premiums are deductible. You can receive a quote online or use an agent. Contact eHealthInsurance.com, BuyerZone.com, or some carriers directly: Blue Cross Bluecares.com, GoldenRule.com, Celtic-net.com, UnitedHealthCare.com, Ask your CPA for a referral if you want to compare an agent's offer. You may save by retaining some level of the risks in the business. Using a self-insurance co-op, you participate with businesses like your own to save money. Some firms form co-ops to rent a captive insurance entity to lower the cost.

There has been an outbreak of medical plan fraud especially by sellers to small business owners. Verify that the insurer is licensed in your state. Based upon recent reports, employers do not find out about the scam until large employee claims are filed. By then, the thieves are long gone. NAIC.org Seniors can compare plans to traditional Medicare at Medicare.gov. Medicare helps you find the insurers who offer Medigap plans in your area. Also contact AARP.com (800-523-5800) for options. If you are retiring from a company that has retiree health, compare it to Medigap plans.

Drugs sold in America are at least twice as expensive as in the rest of the world. Minnesota (state.mn.us) recently made it easy to order drugs from Canada by listing all the prices from approved pharmacies. Compare the federal plans medicare.gov/find-a-plan/questions/home.aspx to AARP.org guidelines. Our taxes pay for drug R&D, not the drug firms in most cases. See **Our Daily Meds** by Melody Petersen for the whole story.

You may be able to save on the generic equivalent of your prescription. Research its effectiveness. Just because the FDA approves a drug does not make it safe. Compare OregonRX.org, CRbestbuydrugs.org, and Aarp.org. Caveat Emptor--"let the buyer beware".

Other medical services, including vision and dental, are usually not worth buying as part of your monthly medical policy premium. One member solved this problem for her family by signing up for coverage for one year. After each family member received their eye and dental needs during the year, the extras were cancelled. Two years later, the member signed up again for another round of services. However, for emergency root canal, the member had to dip into their **Wealth Reserve**™.

Job-hunting time is made more stressful because you lose your coverage too. Employer-sponsored benefits are usually available to you to buy under COBRA when you leave your job. This arrangement seems like a good regulation that business must comply with until you receive the price. Your employer is NOT doing you a favor after all. The price is not the group rate but the full price plus a fee for the employer's trouble. COBRA coverage is priced for the insurance company's benefit, not yours. Find a temporary policy using the sites above. Or go "naked" as the insurance industry calls it, until you find a job.

The critical policy elements

- ✓ If policy renewal isn't guaranteed, you may not have coverage when you get sick.
- ✓ Find a comfortable balance between deductible and catastrophe-only coverage.
- ✓ If you are in good health, medical questions save you money. If not, see bad health.
- ✓ Select a company with high financial strength ("A+").
- ✓ Automatic premium payment from your credit card or bank prevents policy lapse.
- ✓ Application as signed becomes part of the legal contract. Changes must be signed.
- ✓ You are covered by the policy according to the terms of the initial conditional receipt.
- ✓ Sickness coverage may require a probationary period before taking effect.

What to do if you have bad health

✓ If you have a major illness, ask an experienced agent. "Your application and denial are shared at MIB.com. Your association or union may offer a group policy that doesn't cost more. Bluecares.com and state insurance departments have "high risk pool" information. See NASCHIP

✓ If you have just left your job or school, you may convert your group policy without testing.

✓ Your business may qualify for MET or MEWA group coverage. Ask your Chamber of Commerce, accountant, or attorney or Self-employed sites. Ask about HIPAA policies.

A carrier that specializes in your situation may be the best value. A study of people with poor health, "How accessible is individual health insurance for consumers in less-than-perfect health?" found that 90% of the time, the less-healthy hypothetical health insurance applicants in the study were unable to buy policies from individual insurers at standard rates, while 37% of them were rejected outright. Of the 63% who were accepted, most had benefit restrictions placed on them (28%), premium surcharges (13%) or both (12%).

Another study says that even 'f you're in perfect health, you may face barriers to getting a policy based on your age. The premiums for the study's hypothetical healthy 62-year-old man were three to six times higher for him than for their hypothetical healthy 24-year-old woman. If you have a health condition, lying on the application won't help even if you were just covered by another policy. All the records are known to every insurer's clerk around the world even if you guard your privacy.

Companies know that the sickest 1% of insured people use 50% of the claim dollars. There is evidence to suggest that some people are already putting off treatment for fear of being penalized. Other people seek treatment but pay cash and ask for the doctor to not write anything down.

Under a recent health privacy act, all prescription data at your pharmacy can be (and was) sold to the drug companies so that they can send letters to you reminding you to buy more. The government thought that this was a good regulation because parts of the act require that you give your permission before your data is shared with others. However, you did not give your permission for the pharmacy data to be sold to the drug firms. One member received a letter on CVS letterhead but paid for by GlaxoSmithKline mentioning the drug by name. Now, even the postman knows which drugs the member is on. <u>Uncle Sam now buys your data</u> with your tax dollars.

Your final option may be to find a job that provides coverage. High-cost states like MA, NJ and NY leave you with few alternatives. Even part-timers may qualify as full-timers for insurance coverage.

How carriers decide to insure you

- ✓ Every detail about you is data for the underwriter to decide.
- ✓ Your doctor's statement. Let the doctor know in advance.
- ✓ Choice of deductible and co-payment: Fewer large claims are preferred.
- ✓ Timing: Carriers have marketing quotas for preferred insureds per state.
- ✓ Your policy should arrive 4-6 weeks after the application. Check each element.

The carrier has data about your sex, age, health, lifestyle, occupation, avocation, medical and family history as well as your employment, insurance, credit and driving records. Your application answers must match the records too. A lie on your application is used to deny claims.

All of your doctors may be asked to make a statement. All your medical records might be copied. In order to facilitate a decision, you should call all the doctors' offices to let them know you are seeking insurance from ABC Company.

Underwriters want your premium but they don't want your claims, which could cost $3,000,000 or more. Since you are directing the way money is spent for your own health care now (not your employer), you can make your application more attractive to the insurer by picking a large deductible. This form of self-insurance, using your **Wealth Reserve**™, tells the carrier that you will share the burden.

You Have Rights

Individual (not group) health insurance policy provisions adopted by most states.

- An agent cannot modify your contract (application, endorsements and attachments). Changes must be written parts of the contract and signed by an officer of the insurer not the agent.
- Unless your misstatements are fraudulent, the policy becomes incontestable after two years. Claims cannot be denied or reduced because your condition was preexisting.
- You have a grace period with full coverage, if your premium is late, unless you received a non-renewal notice.
- If a policy is lapsed, it is usually reinstated if the agent or company accepts payment, unless a re-application is required. You're reinstated on the 45th day unless it's denied. There is a 10-day waiting period for illness coverage (none for accident).
- You have 20 days to notify the agent or carrier of a loss.
- The carrier has 15 days to give you the forms to prove the loss.
- You must give written proof of loss within 90 days of the accident or disability, unless you are incapacitated. All proofs must be completed within one year.
- Benefits are payable immediately upon receipt of proof. Consult policy for waiting period, if any.
- Death benefits are payable to the beneficiary or the estate of the insured.
- Optional: Relative can be paid up to $1,000 instead of the estate or minor beneficiary.

Optional: Medical provider can be paid the benefits to facilitate payments to insured. The insurer can examine you while you receive benefits or have autopsy performed. You can only sue the insurer 60 days after the loss proof is due (up to 3 years). You can change the beneficiary or re-assign the benefits unless it's irrevocable. If you are rejected, obtain a written explanation so you can fight it.

The agent is required to tell you about the all policy limitations before you sign.

You can change inaccurate medical information the MIB.com provides to the carrier.

Optional policy provisions insurers MAY include:

- Your disability benefit may be reduced if you are employed in a more dangerous job.
- Your benefits may be reduced if you misstate your age.
- Your benefits cannot be increased above the company limit even with 2 policies.
- Your benefits cannot be increased by having the same coverage from another carrier.
- Your benefits cannot be increased by having the same coverage from another type.
- Your disability benefits cannot exceed your income by having 2 policies.
- Your benefits can be reduced by the premium you owe if it is unpaid.
- Your policy may be canceled within 5 days of notice sent unless it is non-cancelable. You receive the unused portion of the premium paid when the policy is canceled.
- Your policy provisions must comply with your state's law no matter how written.
- Your policy will not pay if you are engaged in illegal occupations when loss occurs.
- Your policy will not pay if you are using alcohol or narcotics when the loss occurs.
- Your state may prohibit "post-claim underwriting" which is used to cancel coverage after you file a claim. Call a lawyer like sbd-law.com.

EasySheet   **Find out if you have the best coverage**

	Company A	Company B	Company C
Name			

Premium: Annual_ Semi_ Quarter_

	Company A	Company B	Company C
HMO (with POS option)	$	$	$
PPO network with $1,000 deductible and Reimburse 80% of usual charges	$	$	$
PPO network with $2,500 deductible and Reimburse 80% of usual charges	$	$	$
Prescription drugs	$	$	$
Dental or vision	$	$	$
Grand Total	**$**	**$**	**$**

<u>Policy discounts and benefits</u>

	Company A	Company B	Company C
HSA-qualified plan	[ ]	[ ]	[ ]
All non-smokers	[ ]	[ ]	[ ]
No pre-existing limitations	[ ]	[ ]	[ ]
Family medical history good	[ ]	[ ]	[ ]
Group member	[ ]	[ ]	[ ]
Good health	[ ]	[ ]	[ ]
Maximum benefit over $1,000,000	[ ]	[ ]	[ ]
Pretreatment review required	[ ]	[ ]	[ ]
Family deductible	[ ]	[ ]	[ ]
Stop-loss limit under $10,000	[ ]	[ ]	[ ]
Renewal guaranteed	[ ]	[ ]	[ ]

Self-employed individual HD-HSA plan
A client compared traditional PPO with high-deductible PPO
--Deductible: $1,750 / $5,500
--Premium: $5,580 / $2,424
--One preventive care visit: $0 / $0
--Annual Mammogram: $0 / $0
--Generic Prescription Drug: $180 / $360
--Total Annual Cost: $5,760 / $2,784
She saved $3,000 and funded tax-deductible HSA to pay for health care expenses--maximum $5,500 a year.

11

The Insider's Guide to Mutual Funds & Securities: Beware fees

- ✓ Save up to $60,000 in 20 years
- ✓ Drop "services" you don't need.
- ✓ Your fund or broker charges fees even when they loose your money
- ✓ Brokers are salespeople; not unbiased advisors.

Drop "services" that don't increase your wealth

Our Insider worked for a retail Wall Street firm. He confirms what you knew all along: your broker or mutual fund makes a profit on your relationship whether they help you make money or not. They can't control the market, but you can control their fees and commissions. It is not what you make but what you keep, as the saying goes. There is no proof that a money manager or broker can consistently beat the <u>market</u>, despite the promises. 86% of actively managed mutual funds earn less than the market.
businessweek.com/investing/insights/blog/archives/2009/04/where_have_all.html

The industry charges many commissions and fees (<u>SEC.gov</u>), usually as a percentage of your account total. Fees are taken WHETHER management makes money for you or NOT, whether "<u>service</u>" is good or NOT. jdpower.com/Finance/ratings/full-service-investment-firm-ratings The average total you are paying has risen to <u>1.52%</u> as the industry has grown. The markets have changed. Your total returns are more likely to be worse when you pay a "manager" to manage your money:

> **Saved $30,000**
> Mr and Mrs K of New Jersey transferred all of their mutual fund accounts to the low-cost leader and saved over $3,000 a year in fees. They had been paying 1.2% of their account values each year for 10 years. Their Wealth Reserve will be $545,000 greater because they NOW pay only .20% per year until retirement.

A 2003 study showed that investors continued to make Wall Street rich by chasing returns and trying to time the market's ups and downs. The study found that:

The average investor earned **3.79%; the market earned 11%**

✓ The average equity fund investor earned a paltry **3.79% annually**; compared with 9.14% the S&P 500 index since 1990.
✓ The average fixed income investor earned 1.01% annually; compared to BarclaysAggregate Bond Index return of 6.89%.
✓ It is widely believed that rapid fire trading produces huge profits for traders at the expense of the average investor. But a study shows that market timers actually lose money instead of making healthy profits.
dalbar.com/Portals/dalbar/cache/News/PressReleases/pressrelease040111.pdf

Why do we keep paying more and getting less? Our Insider of 20 years says there are two problems.

1 Paying too much for basic services.
2 Paying for the myth of professional management.

The solution to both problems is available. We can easily learn the secrets of our financial world AND low-cost brokers and funds are now available to all. We can now manage our own investments thanks to discount brokers, ETF and mutual funds. We can even escape taxes with a Roth IRA. Unlike sex education, the basic facts of life—financial **life**— are still not taught to us as teens. Without the facts, we fall prey to the myths of Wall Street.

> "Professional money management is a gigantic rip-off."
> Bill Gross, star bond manager
> *Everything You've Heard about Investing is Wrong*

You may enjoy the friendship of your broker, banker, or insurance agent. Unfortunately, these salespeople usually don't let us know there are better alternatives to the same type of investments without high fees. Usually this salesperson is not the right person to offer us information on similar products without fees. They depend on the fees for food and shelter. A typical $10,000 transaction provides their firm with revenue of $200 to $5,000 depending on the product. Brokers are expected to bring in at least $100,000 a DAY. They keep less than 30% of the revenue. They are fired if they don't keep selling products for the firm.

Our Insider of 20 years points out that it costs less to run a mutual fund and brokerage firm now than it did 20 years ago.

However, the industry *raised* fees and profits. Most mutual fund companies continue to charge 5.75% commission plus 1.5% a year. Many kick back transaction fees and perks to the brokers to keep the business coming their way.
aboutbrokerfraud.typepad.com/about_broker_fraud_blog/kickbacks/.
As these funds get larger, they become high-cost index funds because they have to invest their $656 billion in the same large businesses that make up the market index. Most funds have returned less than 10% over the last 20 years. Vanguard.com's 500 Index has returned over 10% since 1976 without the commissions. Fidelity's Magellan Fund now lags this index because of its fees. As a whole, the industry returned 9% to investors for the period. You could have saved 2% of your account value or $3,000 on a $150,000 portfolio. See Chapter 2 above.

Our members, Mr. and Mrs. K. of New Jersey, transferred all of their mutual fund accounts to the low-cost leader, Vanguard and saved over $3,000 a year in management fees. They were paying about 1.2% of their current account values of $349,000 each year for the last 15 years. That was $4,188 of the current value. Now they pay less than 0.20% or $698 per year. Their retirement fund will be $545,000 greater because they pay 0.2% instead of 1.2% per year until retirement. Compare your present fund to a low-cost leader to see the difference at Vanguard.com.

It does NOT cost $50 or $30 to for your broker to buy or sell securities and send you a statement, which just obscures what you paid in fees anyway. Few show "annual return" or total costs for trading, management and brokerage staff. However, a few mutual funds and discount brokers have actually reduced costs, some to $0 per trade. They put their clients first. Our members use them and save $3,000 or more a year.

Investing directly through these low-cost firms has become routine for those who are comfortable with their goals and investing strategy. If your investing needs are clear, you can earn the maximum amounts on your money by buying services directly from these firms. You can earn higher returns on your retirement, college funding, savings and investment dollars and you can pay the least for quality products by shopping via the Internet or phone.

How to earn 11%; not 3.79%

We can learn how to become successful investors from the people who are successful. Our members are like the financially independent millionaires in **The Millionaire Next Door**. They do not buy and sell securities. They do not follow salespeople's advice. They make their own decisions. They usually hold securities for many years. They have income from multiple sources: business, securities, rental real estate. nytimes.com/books/first/s/stanley-millionaire.html

Did you notice that the number of millionaires rose to 8 million in 2004, increasing 33% over 2003, a banner year for the market? The primary reason was **NOT** smart stock trading. "Most of the new millionaires had made *few* changes to their portfolios since 2000," according to *Money*, March 2005.

Our Insider says that the people who actually reach their goals let TIME do the work. As Warren Buffett, one of the world's best investors put it, "We continue to make more money when snoring than when active." Berkshirehathaway.com/letters/1996

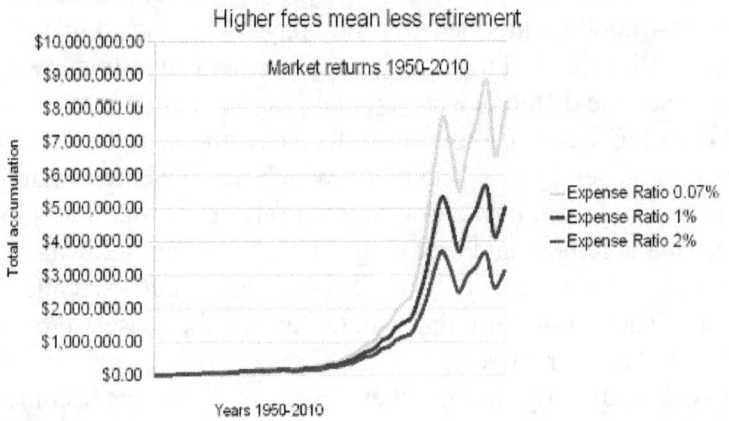

Actually, you can earn higher returns by NOT picking the top stocks and funds. You are buying high. A buy-and-hold strategy tends to maximize your savings and investing dollars over time. A low-cost fund or discount brokerage account helps you earn more by reducing your costs. It is as simple as that. You can earn 11% and **keep 11%** or only 3.79% as the average investor. We suggest you cut out the middle person and skip their advice to buy the "hot" one. You win, they lose.

Of course the industry will dispute that it is just that simple. The industry only makes money when ***they*** touch your money. The Wall Street myth is that you can't be successful in reaching your goals without their "professional management." The industry highlights the positive star mutual funds and fast-moving stocks, and hides the negative: most managed funds earn 2% less than the market indexes. Most traders lose their money to the industry owners who provide the means of losing, just like casino owners.

Is it really worth learning how the market ***really*** works and using the buy-and-hold strategy? Can it be that simple? Is it worth the effort and discomfort to switch brokers or mutual funds to save? **You bet it is!** For instance, by using a low-cost mutual fund family like Vanguard, you earn 1-2% more on your nest egg or college fund. Over time, the value of compounding an extra 2% mounts up. Over time, compounding at an average of 12% versus 10% can improve your lifestyle dramatically.

There aren't many funds that can consistently beat the market returns of 10%-12% per year. Vanguard's 500 index fund has done it over the last 15, 20 and 30 years—since its start in 1976. In recent years, it increased 29% and fell 22%. No manager knows what the future will bring but isn't it comforting to know that you can invest in the next best thing to a certainty--the American economy. The 500 index fund holds the largest 500 firms and you can own a share of all of them! Or buy other indexes of the markets (Callan.com). We explained how to do this above.

Thus, smart investors avoid the anxiety-producing hunt for the best fund or stock. **There is none!** Each quarter the best changes. With a low-cost index fund, at least you know you don't overpay. Your funds will **average** 10% per year over 10 years 95% of the time. Can your current fund manager promise that? Low-cost index funds take only $180 per $100,000 account value. Will your current fund manager reduce their $1,500 annual fee when they do a poor job? About 86% of managers produce less than the market averages. Yet we continue to pay them! What a business! ifa.com/12steps/Step3/Step3Page2.asp#333

Actually, Fidelity has decided cost matters so much that it has copied Vanguard's strategy. In 2004, it lowered the fees on some of its index funds to 0.10%. However, before you switch to Fidelity, check the Fidelity.com temporary waiver: "This arrangement may be discontinued at anytime." It is hidden in the second paragraph at the very bottom of the page.

The money you NOW waste can build wealth!

Our members think they can use the extra earnings rather than Wall Street. Members who have become financially independent say they wish they had learned how to buy and hold low-cost market- 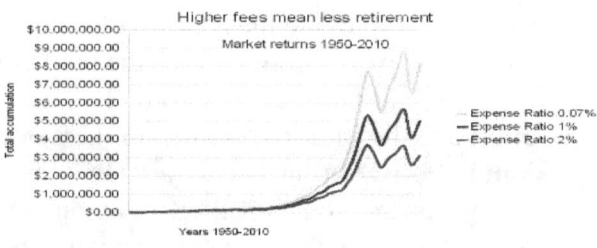 average funds earlier in their lives. Apparently, more people are learning because Vanguard's index funds are among the largest funds in the world, despite the fact that **no** broker, agent or banker sells them!

    Members believe that their saving and investing dollars should go DIRECTLY into low-cost mutual funds or index funds traded like stocks (Exchange-Traded Funds or ETF's). Avoid middle persons' fees. Our members share their experiences with indexes in Chapter 2. You find out which securities are recommended by super investors Warren Buffett, Peter Lynch, and Charles Schwab. finance.yahoo.com/etf/education

    Successful investor members have their fund manager AUTOMATICALLY debit a monthly amount from their checking accounts. Stock mutual funds help you reach long-term goals like college and retirement funding. Balanced mutual funds can provide cash for all your short-term spending like cars, vacations and emergencies. A balanced (stocks and bonds) mutual fund can compound at 6-8% with fewer ups and downs.
personal.vanguard.com/us/funds/snapshot?FundId=0056&FundIntExt=INT

    So, investing $250 a month, $3,000 annually for 5 years can compound to $17,500; $50,000 in 10 years. Then you can write a check to buy a vehicle, vacation, or home down payment. To estimate how much you can accumulate, use
Moneychimp.com/calculator/compound_interest_calculator. The Insider Guides help you decide to re-direct your current spending on financial services in order to **generate that extra $250 a month to**

build your Wealth Reserve™.

Some members use the savings on mutual funds and securities' fees to pay cash for their cars, appliances, vacations, and other goals painlessly. They have built a **Wealth Reserve**™ already. Mr and Mrs K are now celebrating their best years of earnings by cashing in some of their mutual fund shares to buy a vacation home at the Jersey shore.

Our members are using a self-funding strategy for the things they use up, like cars, appliances, and vacations. When you borrow to buy assets that don't grow in value, the cost can be FIVE times the price. The benefit of this strategy is to have your income grow your wealth using compound interest. Building this **Wealth Reserve**™ protects you against giving money away to banks, especially the $3,000 to $4,000 in interest most people pay every year on credit cards and car loans.

Instead, the $3,000 buys assets that "grow by themselves." You avoid giving your hard-earned money to the banker, broker or agent. Making your money work for 10 years in your **Wealth Reserve**™ can provide about $51,000—enough for a home down payment, car, vacation, etc. You will have paid only $30,000 ($3,000 for 10 years) for that $51,000. The difference is the "miracle of compounding." courses.dsu.edu/finance/retire.htm

You don't have to make a budget or "tighten your belt."

Our strategy works because you don't have to *find* the money to build your **Wealth Reserve**™. You use the money you already spend for financial services that you decide you don't really need. Instead of buying a car or appliance and paying **5 times** the price (financing costs plus the money you did not earn with compounding), you pay "compounded" cash (the $51,000 described above cost you only $30,000!). You pay less because you planned ahead. See our Insider's Guide to Banking to avoid paying five times the price.

The savings explained in our Insider's Guides provide the money to grow your **Wealth Reserve**™. Then you can use your Reserve for all major purchases. You turn the amounts that you usually pay the financial services providers into enough money to pay cash for all your needs. You use your income to buy "assets that grow by themselves," not pay fees and interest to make others very wealthy. The recommendations in this Insider's Guide assume that you have or will put your **Wealth Reserve**™ growth on automatic. You can forget it once you start it.

There are many choices in the level of brokerage or mutual fund services you can buy today. You can make your broker rich by picking up the phone and asking what to do with your saving and investing money. Your banker, broker or agent is a salesperson. This nice person is going to offer you the best commission-laden package they have to sell. They won't offer you the best value package because their **firm** doesn't even offer it. Salespeople don't pick the products they sell. The institution picks the products based upon the kickbacks, soft-dollar and other benefits it obtains from the manufacturers. Fidelity brokers were pressured to sell Fidelity products and some quit: investmentnews.com/apps/pbcs.dll/article?AID=/20090403/REG/904039959

The last thing a salesperson wants you to do is understand products they don't offer. This is why services are sold as a bundle of services. Very few customers change their initial relationship. The brokerage firm is counting on you NOT shopping for your products/services un-bundled from a low-cost provider. We think you don't need your traditional bank, broker or agent in the 21st century. Think about what that $3,000 a year can do for you—NOT them. You could be giving away **half a million dollars or more in earnings over time.**

The more you buy of what the salesperson recommends, the more you and they feel you have a "great" relationship. Our members have learned not to buy what is offered. They have learned what they need, not what the salesperson has to sell. When our Insider worked with Wall Street brokers, he noticed that most of them couldn't focus on more than 3 products at a time. The firm decides what those three products are. stockbroker-fraud.com/lawyer-attorney-1133786.html The industry mantra is "products are sold not bought." This means there are better alternatives available but they don't pay commissions. Through greed or fear, you are sold them.

Check your firm and broker with the FINRA.org.

For instance, New Hampshire securities regulators have accused the personal finance advisory unit of American Express of defrauding investors by giving incentives to its advisers to push select mutual funds over other funds with better performance. sos.nh.gov/securities/Press_Releases/PRESSR_2005-02-18.pdf

Our Insider's Guides help you save money by explaining the high-value services you need. The seller wants you to buy the package as presented and leave the details to them. Our members do the opposite: they buy only what they need.

Advice is the most important benefit

Advice is the most important benefit most people say they pay a broker to provide. However, most don't give good advice. Also, if you have a financial strategy, you don't really need a salesperson in the 21st century. You can have your investing dollars go to your **Wealth Reserve**™ automatically. You can obtain your statement online anytime and at least once a quarter. You guarantee that your spending plan will be accomplished when you invest automatically. Your emotions are removed from the decisions about your long-term strategy.

Your broker and fund manager are not able to predict the future. The analysts they use can't either. *Forbes* 2006 They can't beat the market consistently. They are paid based upon the *volume* of money they control, not your returns. The manager makes more as the assets grow. A broker's incentive varies widely among products. There are other perks. The more products and deposits and extras that are handled by your salesperson, the larger the incentives and bonuses they receive. Not even the analysts are paid to be right. They are paid on volume too.

Hedge Funds Underperform Index 1996-2003
economist.com

Sales people are trained to handle your objections, not to give you the best alternatives for YOU. They are not in business to provide you with the appropriate service at the least cost. The same services can cost FIVE times as much from one company to the next. Our **EasySheet** below helps you find each service level that is right for you. You can buy low-cost mutual funds and securities by phone or computer in less than 10 minutes DIRECTLY from the manufacturers. Our members have saved $500 in 30 minutes on the Internet. It is safer than sending checks.

This Guide helps you take advantage of our Insider's "tricks of the trade." You probably don't need some services if you evaluate how you use brokerage and fund services. To reach your goals, you need to build your **Wealth Reserve**™. You can build your Reserve by earning more on your account balance by eliminating the extra 1.5% fee you pay now. Your Reserve may be $300,000 to $500,000 larger in 20 years just from that **one small change today**. It is more likely that your market index fund will rise further than your manager's stock picks will rise over time. Plus, you don't have to find the right manager every quarter.

Your **Wealth Reserve**™ is your self-funded 'bank' to buy the things you want. You need to make a plan so that the money will be there when you need it. You can have the money that grew by itself in your **Wealth Reserve**™ because you stopped paying commissions, fees, and interest to your banker, broker, and agent. Start earning cash on your income. You become a creditor not a debtor; a "banker" not a borrower.

WARNING: This Guide offers advice on how to self-fund your needs. This Guide shows you how to drop services you may not need. However, before you change your money manager, make certain that the alternative plan is in place. Do not close the old account until you have tried the services from your new providers and started your **Wealth Reserve**™.

Let's talk about the services you really need and where to buy them for less. If you agree that you want to maximize the earning power of your income, then you need to earn money on as much of your monthly income as possible. You need to grow your **Wealth Reserve**™ even when rates and returns are low. You have your choice of investments that provide earnings no matter what the state of the economy. Your employer's 401k may be your one and only investment vehicle. Some employers even give you FREE money to belong. **Take it!**

Do you participate in your employer's retirement (401k, 403b, pension, profit-sharing) plan? Over half of those who are eligible do not. Since many employers match your contributions to some extent, you are throwing money away if you don't accept it. You should consider this money as part of your salary.
http://www.401khelpcenter.com/2011_401k_plan_limits.html

Some Network members contribute to their employer's plan even though they don't receive matching funds. They receive

TAX-DEFERRAL on contributions up to $17,000 in 2013 (401k) plus $5,500 more if over 50 years of age and they lower their current taxable income. Tax-deferral allows your money to grow faster since there are no taxes to pay NOW. This benefit of qualified plans can mean an extra $570,000 over 30 years (annual investment of $3,000, earning a fixed 10% return compounded monthly).

The flaw in employer tax-deferred plans is the cost structure, which *you* must bear. If your employer has not been careful in selecting a low-cost provider, you can get skinned. The mutual fund company may charge its regular fees plus extra fees to pay for the employer's record keeping and pension consultant. Some mutual funds may be rebating part of the fees you pay back to the plan administrator, according to the SEC.gov in July 2004. Some overpay brokers. The extra costs mean you have 14% to 25% less in retirement. Fees range from 0.35% to 1.72%.

Some members have provided cost comparison information to their HR department at work in order to show how much money is lost. See brightscope.com/ratings/. Our President and Congress people have the best deal. Their index funds (tsp.gov Thrift Savings Plan) charge just 0.05%. Plus, they mandate that those responsible for running the funds be leaders in their fields.

Unfortunately, some plans offer poor investment options and high fees and quarterly or annual charges for all participants. Those with lower salaries pay a disproportionate share of the accounting costs for the plan. The original sales person and the fund management continue to reap huge mark-ups on the assets over 30 or 40 years. Again you may be paying $3,000 a year in fees that rob you of thousands in retirement dollars. One member pays $30 plus 2.49% per year on zero growth since 1999. Her company picked Mass Mutual. If she leaves her job, she must pay 9% surrender charge to transfer money to a rollover IRA.

If you have a choice of investments, consider the cost of the funds you pick. We advocate that you put all your retirement plan money in stock index funds. They are usually the least expensive. Your employer's retirement plan should not be your only investment choice. Avoid buying only company stock. Chapter 2 explains how our members have reached their short-term and long-term goals. There are options that complement your work plan and are TAX-FREE. A **Wealth Reserve**™ with low-cost funds may be a cheaper option because earnings are tax-FREE. Taxes and fees can take 50% of our plan accumulations. Switching to a low-fee Roth 401k with employer match maximizes compounding.

Buy only the services you need

Your broker, banker, agent or mutual fund firm may *not* provide what you need in the 21st century. Our Insider helps you understand financial costs so you can drop what you don't need. In a sentence, you can save enough money in fees and charges on your financial services in order to buy the things you need by letting your money compound FIRST. You turn the tables on the industry. You keep the compound interest on your money instead of your banker, fund manager and insurer.

The financial industry is specializing. Brokers and funds can't earn a profit on your accounts unless you have big balances with them. If you want to become financially independent, decide what you need and buy it directly from the low-cost providers.

If your long-term goals can be met by earning 12% on your long-term money, then you don't need a broker or high-fee mutual funds. If your short-term goals can be accomplished by earning 8%-10%, then you don't need a broker or load funds. You are better off with low-cost mutual funds. You don't need investment fees since no money manager can guarantee high-returns.

If your strategy is to buy and sell individual securities that you think may outperform the 12% average, at least with part of your money, be advised: Brokerage firms do not provide the best research and advice because they make money on trade volume not on stock picking prowess. Brokerage firms develop research to support the **selling** of securities they underwrite for really big fees. Things have not changed since the scandal of 2000-2001, according to analyst Matt Murray. oag.state.ny.us New stock issues (IPO's) are provided to their best institutional customers. Our Insider confirms what Ronald Glantz, former director of research and chief investment officer for PaineWebber (now UBS), told the House.gov back in August 2001.

[Stock] analysts used to view retail customers and investment managers as their clients. Now, the job of analysts is to bring in investment banking clients, **not provide good investment advice**. This began in the mid-1980s. The prostitution of security analysts was completed during the high-tech mania of the last few years.

The financially savvy do NOT listen to the 'experts' because the experts are usually paid to promote certain stocks, not give wise advice. A study by Investars shows how poorly Wall Street firms would do if they *actually followed their own advice*. Nineteen brokerage recommendations were followed from January 1997 to June 2001 while an index of the largest 500 companies gained 75%.

If Wall Street actually took its own advice!

The average return for the top 10 brokerage firms **was *minus* 2.26%** from 1997-2001! Most were negative. If you owned shares of a low-cost index fund, you would have been ahead 75%. Products are "sold not bought" for a reason!

Savvy asset buyers know that stock analysts and brokerage firms pick stocks they can benefit from praising. As we heard from one of the analysts, Mr. Glantz, above, the analysts promote what their own firms sell. Careers and bonuses are *not* made by being correct forecasters--helping *you* get rich--but by generating revenue for their firms. Things haven't changed as Matt Murray tells in the *NYTimes*, 4/9/6. Bloomberg found S&P 500 companies with the most "buy" ratings gained 8.7 percent in 2010, while the ones with the fewest "buys" jumped 20 percent.

Members who do buy and sell securities use discount brokers AFTER they do their own research. They use discount brokers to make the transactions. They use sites like AAII.com, Morningstar.com, Yahoo.com and Reuters.com to learn about and screen ETF and stocks of companies for possible purchase. Typically they buy and hold quality companies they are familiar with. They have spent hours learning about these firms and the industry. Some hold very few securities. These are just one asset class among many that they own. They like the idea of not "putting all their eggs in one basket."

They use the Internet and their own accountants and lawyers to investigate investments. Like the *Millionaire*[s] *Next Door*, our members do not speculate on stocks or funds. Typically, they do not try to time the market by buying the hot sector or country funds. Some use Modern Portfolio Theory to increase returns as they reduce risk. They illustrate what they do above.

Consider why many savvy investors continue to stuff money into the top 10 no-load mutual funds—most of which are not advertised or promoted: http://www.500indexfund.com/. Are these millions of investors stupid for not listening to their brokers? Compare your total return to these funds.

Some members invest in long-term trends like health-care, age-related recreation, and housing. For instance, one member thinks that the baby-boomer generation will continue to buy RV equipment in order to enjoy travel in North America at their own pace. The member owns the stock of Thor and reads the company reports and information filed with the SEC, as well as industry sites and investor sites like Yahoo and Reuters. Disclaimer: One of our Insiders owned Thor. We are not advocating Thor.

Discount brokers are not created equal. Some have good rates for purchasing a quantity of securities, a set dollar amount per month or a set fee to trade anytime or to buy or sell at set times during the day. Depending on your needs, you can buy securities for as little as $0, with some restrictions. You may have an annual fee. Most firms offer automatic monthly purchases and dividend reinvestment. broker-reviews.us/

However, if you only want to buy the stock of one company on a regular basis, you may be able to cut out the brokerage altogether. You can buy directly from the company. Check all the strings attached at Enrolldirect now us.computershare.com/. Few corporations offer no cost plans.

If you are thinking, "this is a great idea for stocks; what about bonds;" you can buy our government's bonds at TreasuryDirect.gov. You can buy CDs and bonds wholesale at ZionsDirect.com. Recently investors have been offered new corporate bonds paying interest monthly. See Internotes.com.

If "preferred" rates on CDs are your "investments" of choice, you need to shop around. Brokers can make $150 on the CD's they sell you. You can use CD's to maximize your fixed income returns, especially when rates are rising. See our Insider's Guide to Banking to find higher rates.

Brokers now offer mortgages. Mortgage rates are determined by your credit and a buy-down rate (points). You can be overcharged on closing fees. We think you can do better by dealing directly with a mortgage specialist. We help you buy the mortgage you need with our Insider's Guide to Mortgages. If you need money from your home, a home equity line or reverse mortgage may help you.

Borrowing from your broker (margin account) to buy securities is tricky and expensive. If you really believe that your broker can foretell the future and thus borrowing will bring you a windfall, please see the film *Boiler Room* first. imdb.com/

Brokers also offer fee-based accounts. You can trade securities for a fixed fee up to 2.5% depending on the size of your account. Even though your broker has no incentive to churn your account, the firm still rewards the broker for selling certain products. Plus heavy trading doesn't guarantee gains. Most studies show the opposite—your expenses exceed gains.

Another fee-based system called "wrap accounts" claims your money is "managed" by famous managers. However, you will pay dearly for the promise (not fact) of good management. You pay a huge fee, up to 3.5%, whether you make money or not. Usually the minimums are $100,000 so you drop $3,500 or more every year, guaranteed. These managers use models, not your needs, to pick your portfolio, according to our Insider.

The mutual fund wraps are less expensive versions of the promise of higher earnings. Savvy investors don't fall for this one. They go directly to low-cost providers. See members' real asset allocations in Chapter 2.

Many brokerage firms offer single statement cash management accounts, which provide a way to manage all you assets on one platform. Again beware of the fees. Low-cost providers like Vanguard.com and TRowePrice.com also offer this benefit at low cost. You can have your check-writing and ATM card account in one place too. Some discount brokers link your account to an Internet-only bank.

If you rely on a broker to do transactions, keep a copy of all your forms, instructions, confirmations and statements. Take notes of your conversations. We have found that members who ran into mistakes were better off in disputes because they had copious notes. Usually you can only have a hearing with an industry arbitration specialist. You can't sue a broker.

You will notice there are fees for almost everything a broker offers. For instance, if you want a real certificate of a security sent to you, you will pay. It is inconvenient to store and ship certificates yourself.

Monthly fees for a low balance can cost you $1,800 over the years. If you find you have to pay this fee often, it is time to switch account types or brokers. Some brokers offer free accounts to start but add fees later. Some deep discount brokers charge fees if you hold small amounts, especially in IRA accounts.

This Guide helps you take advantage of our Insider's 'tricks of the trade'.

Research and advice from your broker may be your reason for paying higher fees. Now you can receive the information yourself automatically. You can download all the reports that your favorite company has to file with the SEC.gov yourself. You can read press releases and news from Yahoo.com and Reuters.com about your favorite companies automatically BEFORE your broker can send them to you. Brokers rarely have special information just for you. Martha Stewart found out why. Brokers are there to sell you, not advise you.

Buy only the services you need

1. Mutual funds for long-term accumulation: Vanguard.com and Fidelity.com provide stock and bond funds at the lowest costs. TIAA-CREF.org and USAA.com offer lower initial investment minimums. Most of these firms offer automatic investing and a full range of products including other mutual funds, individual securities and cash management features such as no-minimum, unlimited check writing and online bill payment. Some offer financial planning and fee-only advisors of top quality at low cost.

2. Brokerage with a purpose. You control your buying strategy with deep discount brokers. Pay the least cost and pick only the services you really need. BuyandHold.com, Scottrade.com, Zecco.com and ING's ShareBuilder.com each have a pricing plan to fit your needs. They may offer a full range of mutual funds and cash management features also. See below.

3. Some brokerage firms charge less if you buy and sell selected ETF and stocks at certain times of the day. Thus BuyandHold

charges $2.99 per IRA trades of popular securities only three times a day. Zecco.com offers a wider range of securities in real time for $0—FREE with conditions. See BrokerReviews.us.

4. Full service brokerage firms offer the flush investor all the personal services needed to conduct extravagant lifestyles globally. This includes personal and commercial mortgage, lending, and investment banking. These firms pride themselves on being able to serve countries and their potentates. Financially independent people usually can accomplish their goals without the fees and scandals required by this kind of firm. They will hold hands.

5. Hedge funds are for gamblers. Since the minimums are high and there are only guaranteed costs, consider the odds: 25% fail each YEAR. "Hedge fund investors would have been better off buying an S&P500 Index," according to a recent study. businessinsider.com/hedge-funds-the-emperors-new-clothes-2011-7#ixzz1R40JDlVJ study (economist.com) found that they did worse than the market. Enough said.

Find the BEST **value** based upon your needs.

- Internet-only brokers don't have the expenses of branch staff and fancy buildings.
- Mutual funds without private owners can provide lower costs and good service.

Investing in the 21st century starts with establishing your own **Wealth Reserve**™. This becomes your lifetime investment portfolio to reach your goals. It can also become your 'bank' for buying things you would normally finance with credit. We are more likely to outlive our money than die, so we are working longer hours. Bls.gov

By investing your income automatically in a portfolio of securities or funds monthly, you can maximize your total wealth without extra money or time or broker. By using low-cost methods like index funds, you can reach your long-term goals like retirement funding and pay for appliances, vacations, and luxury cars when you need them at the lowest cost. Credit cards and loans

ROB you of your future **compounded asset growth** because you often pay up to **FIVE** times the price of the item. You can accomplish all of your goals by buying "assets that grow by themselves," online directly.

Investing has changed. Brokers are trying to take control of your "asset-management" business, which is extremely profitable. Most brokers or mutual fund managers do not offer the best products in this area. For instance, index mutual funds cost little to run because the manager just holds (not trades) a set list of securities. However, some of the most expensive index funds are sold by banks and insurers.

For instance, one insurance company charged 1.29% per year plus 3% contingency fee for the same performance that Fidelity offers for only 0.10%. That is THIRTEEN times the price for the same thing. You could gain $1.1M for retirement at the low cost provider versus only $0.88M for the same $250 a month over 31 years. Beware of <u>fee</u>s.
mba.yale.edu/news_events/CMS/Articles/5530.shtml

Each broker, banker and agent dreams of capturing 100% of your financial spending. Your friendly banker, broker, and agent want to sell you every financial product they have to sell even if it is not the best for your financial health. The Internet has made it easier for you to buy the best of what you need. Financially-independent people find better value for their money from firms that specialize. We think that you can find better value by comparing costs and not giving your entire "portfolio" to any salesperson.

The unsung heroes of investing are the mutual fund families that are customer-focused. Only a few firms proved whom they really care about during the 2003 scandal. Vanguard, TIAA-CREF and USAA are operated without a separate owner. Other fund families offer low-cost investments but may be tempted to increase the bottom line by special trading deals. The <u>Attorney General</u> of New York, put it this way:

The full extent of this complicated fraud is not yet known. But one thing is clear: The mutual fund industry operates on a double standard. Certain companies [Bank of America's Nations Funds, Banc One, Janus and Strong] and individuals have been given the opportunity to manipulate the system. They make illegal after-hours trades and improperly exploit market swings in ways that harm ordinary long-term investors.

oag.state.ny.us

Governance of the company that owns the funds is THE real issue. At least we know the mission of the three mutual fund firms above.

Vanguardcom Group is owned by its shareholders—NOT a management company, like Fidelityholding $1 trillion assets for institutions and individuals. Vanguard offers funds with the lowest operating expenses: $20 for each $10,000 compared with $205 per year for the industry.

TIAA.org is the world's largest pension manager, primarily for educational and research institutions. With $435B in assets, this organization now offers its low-cost products, with the highest service quality, to individuals too. TIAA holds the highest ratings from the four rating agencies.

USAA.com is a diversified financial services institution owned by its members—armed services personnel and you. Since it is a member-owned organization, without capital stock, serving members is its only concern. It has won many service awards.

Most of our members have found that the least expensive discount broker and the least expensive mutual fund family allow them to maintain total control of their multiple asset portfolios. They enjoy market returns of 10%-12% overall but also like to buy individual issues of companies for which they have special knowledge. These members maintain index funds for broad exposure to the markets and concentrate part of their portfolios in areas that they know well. They know more about some firms than a broker ever will.

Members know that costs are important. You can benefit by shopping for the services you need. The Internet helps you find the broker or fund with the lowest cost for your needs. We think this is better than buying from a broker who calls you. It is easier to know what you want now. The self-funded customer, with a **Wealth Reserve**™ growing larger every month, will find this is the best way to buy the services they need.

The best value for you may be a firm that provides you with special benefits due to your occupation, associations, or situation. For those who qualify, USAA provides brokerage, banking and credit cards. USAA has no agents or offices, yet provides such good service that the industry uses its "best in class" models of processing and service excellence. It was named Best by *Worth* magazine readers.

Many traditional brokers are getting into the act by offering online brokerage services. Most have fees. Most require a substantial relationship to pay for the bricks and mortar too. Direct-to-customer brokers and mutual fund firms are growing and can make it easy for you to interact with them in the way you find convenient. You can invest automatically or by computer in less than 10 minutes. Members think that many of these firms are safer than traditional brokers.

Shop for low-cost investing services

✓ Save $3,000 per year by using customer-focused mutual funds: Vanguard.com, TIAA-CREF.org, USAA.com. (Fidelity is owned by the Johnson family.)
✓ Shop brokers for every need. BuyandHold.com, TradeKing.com, Scottrade.com, ShareBuilder.com, TDAmeriTrade.com, Etrade.com, Zecco.com, Schwab.com are just the ones our members have used. Beware inactivity fees—e.g. $40.00/quarter, with many exemptions. Discount.broker-reviews.us
✓ Before buying individual bonds, check the prices at Investinginbonds.com, Municipalbonds.com, FINRAbondinfo.com. Research stocks and ETF's at Morningstar.com, FinanceYahoo.com, AAII.com, Reuters.com, or your broker's site. Thrifty members are rewarded by using TreasuryDirect.gov. Check Finance.yahoo.com/etf for ETF's.
✓ Individual securities can also be purchased directly from the companies. See stock1.com/map-bsd.htm or call the companies directly to compare transaction fees. Sec.gov/answers/drip.htm
✓ Earn 8 to 12% mini-lending to people directly. Prosper.com and LendingClub.com are pending. Diversify your assets.

Compare at least three institutions for price and service with our *EasySheet* below.

For bond buyers, full-service brokers may be looking to clean out their inventories and thus already have the bond you want in stock.

Firms like Fidelity may charge less commission (even less online), but may have a higher markup to cover the cost of buying the one you want. Edward Jones was rated high by JD Power.

You may be better off with new bond issues only. Some issues have huge markups and some can't be sold easily if you need cash. Some brokers have access to new issues. Some do not. If you are going to trade bonds, you need an experienced broker with inventory at a big firm.

You may find excellent value by buying Treasuries directly and keeping them to maturity. I bonds may be your best buy in a falling interest market. An annuity without a surrender charge can offer another alternative. See our Insider's Guide to Annuity Products. Our Insider can help with your Retirement Spending Plan too.

Internet brokers are convenient and safe

We recommend you consider using an Internet broker for your securities. Unless you are a professional gambler/trader, you can pay substantially less in fees and commissions over the years. Most members buy and hold stocks so brokers are moving them out of their account books. It just makes sense. Brokers don't make money if you invest wisely: buy and hold.

SAFETY is a key issue. Most have the same SIPC insurance as traditional brokers. PROBLEM resolution is the sticking point as it is with any broker. Try using email to ask questions. How long does it take to get an answer? Members complain more about having to go back to their broker again and again to get the same problem fixed. It takes time to go there and wait for a broker's assistant to fix the problem. Check sites like complaints.com, ConsumerAffairs.com, and epinions.com to see what problems happened in the past. AAII.com members use Scottrade more than others.

Critical service elements:

- Select a broker with SIPC insurance.
- Select a broker that will not sell your name and number.
- Select a broker that tells you all the costs up front. Big name

firms are the worst.
- If you're concerned about personal service, some discounters have offices.
- Customer "complaints" indicate quality issues.
- Confirm you have the best deal for the service you actually use.
- Confirm your mutual fund is not a 3-alarm type: http://www.mutualfundobserver.com/Confirm you have all costs disclosed. See our **EasySheet** below.

Caveat Emptor = Buyer Beware!

Brokerage disagreements

Using a brokerage firm requires the involvement of many people. Transactions are not complicated but salespeople don't like paperwork. It our experience that every member has had disagreements and problems.
http://www.securitieslaw.com/information/common-complaints.asp

Assume every transaction will get messed up. Most firms accept your money and don't let you sue if there is a problem. investingonline.org Read your account application documents. Our Insider suggests the following:

1. Take the time to put your goals and objectives in writing. Most brokers won't ask for them but this statement can protect you later when things go wrong. Send it to the manager too.
2. Ask what the small print on all forms means. Disagreements go to arbitration not court. The brokerage firm has the advantage. It is better to ask questions now than try to get your money back later. The industry runs the arbitration process.
3. Confirm every order in writing stating what you understand the purpose of the investment is. One member told the broker to sell in 1991 and he did not, even when it was confirmed in writing. Check their record at FINRA.com. The brokerage never made good.
4. Ask the purpose and expected outcome of any trade recommended by the broker.
5. Check your confirms and statements. Fix any error immediately. **Caveat emptor.** Check dates and amounts for tax reporting. After calling, put it in writing. Copy the manager.
6. Take notes of every conversation. Let the broker know you are doing it. You will need documentation when you have a

disagreement. Without notes, you will not win arbitration. Brokers are more careful if they know the conversation is being documented.

7. <u>Beware commissions and fees. Keep track of them in your log for tax returns Ask the broker for a full breakdown. There are fees for everything except broker calls.</u>

8. Insist on a copy of everything. Copy your letters to your broker. Keep literature and anything the broker sends to you.

9. Make the portfolio review a must visit. Discuss the progress you are making toward your goals. Discuss the strategy. Ask for details. Get a written "total return" number annually. Compare it to the appropriate benchmark. You can <u>clear up erroneous information</u> posted to your account.
Investingonline.org/aio/complaintcenter

EasyMove method

This Guide helps you decide which brokerage services you really need. If you have come to the decision that you don't have the best deal, move your account. The best way to do this is gradually.

First. Open the new account.
Second. Ask for help transferring your portfolio from the old firm. You don't need to talk to your old broker. Some funds cannot be moved since they are proprietary. Re-balance assets with the cash.
Third. Contact the old firm's manager by letter. Writing them gives you proof if delays occur.
Fourth. Compare your old statement to your portfolio registry. Have all the assets been transferred?
Fifth. Ask the new firm to help transfer late dividends and checks from your old account. It may take a month or two. Ask for fee reimbursement.

Estimate of how long your portfolio will last

$5,833 per month
Spend 8% of your $500,000 each year
starting at age 65
$3,333 per month plus
Pension and Social Security 2,500 per month
90% chance of funds lasting to age 95
40% Stock, 60% Bond portfolio
(Inflation adjusted)

$4,166 per month
Spend 8% of your $250,000 each year
starting at age 65
$1,666 per month plus
Pension and Social Security 2,500 per month
90% chance of funds lasting to age 95
40% Stock, 60% Bond portfolio
(Inflation adjusted)

Estimates using 1,000 market return simulations at
https://www3.troweprice.com/ric/ricweb/public/ricResults.do
also:
http://www.bankrate.com/calculators/retirement/retirement-plan-income-calculator.aspx
http://cgi.money.cnn.com/tools/retirementplanner/retirementplanner.jsp

EasySheet   Find out if you have the best value:

	Company A	Company B	Company C
Name			

Fees: Annual__ Month__ Per use__
License Check FINRA.org ____   ____   ____

	Company A	Company B	Company C
Regular account			
Market orders	$	$	$
Limit orders	$	$	$
Mutual fund buy/sell fee	$	$	$
Options	$	$	$
Margin rate	%	%	%
Minimum balance required	$	$	$
Minimum to open	$	$	$
Inactivity fee	$	$	$
Tie-in deal or conditions			
Bonus	$	$	$
Conditions	____	____	____
Lower loan rate	%	%	%
Margin account fee	$	$	$
IRA account fee	$	$	$
Close ACATS	$	$	$

Products: Stocks, options, bonds, mutual funds, CDs, muni's, foreign

Benefits:

Credit card with 30-day grace period	____	____	____
Debit card	____	____	____
Bill payment online	____	____	____
Bank account link	____	____	____
Free fund transfer	____	____	____
ATM deposit acceptance	____	____	____
Free dividend reinvestment	____	____	____
Free check writing money market	____	____	____
Free line of credit commitment	____	____	____
SIPC protection	____	____	____
Complaint process checked	____	____	____
Affiliated with other brokerage/bank	____	____	____
Comprehensive statement	____	____	____
Other _____	____	____	____

How to Buy Securities

1. Cost matters: Broker/advisor cost 1% to 3%

    If you use a salesperson, it can cost HALF A NEST EGG!
    $3,000 per year @12% for 33 years = $1,127,324
    $3,000 per year @12-1% for 33 years = $887,525
    $3,000 per year @12-2% for 33 years = $702,083
    $3,000 per year @12-3% for 33 years = $558,284

2. Broker/advisor stock picking does not beat index funds over the long run. No money manager has been able to beat the market consistently. No one can forecast the future.

3. Time is the key to investment success. The chance of you buying AND selling, both, at the right times, is near zero.

4. A Tax-FREE investment account increases your balance 25%.

5. Putting all your money in one stock or market sector guarantees failure over time. No investment is perfect.

6. 'Dollar cost average' buying technique lowers the cost of shares over time. When you invest a fixed amount each month, you buy more shares when the price is low and less when high. Over time, you will own more shares at a lower average cost.

7. "The market is a way to transfer money from the impatient to the **patient**." Warren Buffett

12

The Insider's Guide for Women:
Ensure Your Own Financial Health with Wealth

1. Women are better investors because you have patience
2. Women control family spending when you have a plan
3. A woman's average retirement income can equal a man's
4. Women lose over $600,000 in earnings but can earn $1 million
5. Social Security does not have to be your only source of income
6. You do not have to live below the poverty level

You need to set up a **Wealth Reserve**™ for your own financial health. You need to think about your own future in combination with your family's future. You don't have to end up in Medicaid long-term care facilities like past generations.

Excuses don't count anymore. You NEED to know about money and to start taking control. Do NOT give up financial control when you get married. Make a Spending Plan (next chapter) by tracking every dime for 3 months. You both need to know where your salaries go and why you're not investing 10% for the future. It is never too late do something about it.

First, discuss your feelings with your family. **Second**, get to know how your family invests for retirement. **Third**, build a "**Wealth Reserve**™" to make sure you are protected with "assets that grow by themselves" tax-FREE over time. Some of our members recommend reading *Maxing Out* by Collette Dowling.

As discussed above, your family **Wealth Reserve**™ consists of all the assets you own that "grow by themselves." It allows you to insure and finance yourself instead of giving your hard won income to your broker, banker or agent. Your **Wealth Reserve**™ allows you (and your spouse) to provide for your own permanent "living" insurance, long-term care insurance, and disability insurance coverage, if needed.

Your **Wealth Reserve**™ will provide cash for YOUR retirement funding. If your spouse will receive or does receive a pension, you may be the pension beneficiary. Most pensions provide some fraction of the pre-death benefit to you. However, the amount is usually not enough to ensure that you can continue the same lifestyle as before.

Even if there is a life insurance benefit, at death, a lump sum may not provide for continued income AND a principal large enough to guarantee your long-term health care needs. Establish and fund your own pension at work or by using a **Wealth Reserve**™ §408 trust as suggested above. You must make your own financial future.

Your own **Wealth Reserve**™ may allow you to be financially independent like many of our members. With a strategy to meet your specific long term income needs, you can gain the peace of mind that a large growing asset base can provide. The key is taking action immediately. It is TIME not investment skill that creates a **Wealth Reserve**™. You don't need to be genius stock picker. My favorite quote:

> "We continue to make more money when snoring than when active."
> Warren Buffett, berkshirehathaway.com

Our members have shown that they can build that **Wealth Reserve**™ simply by RE-DIRECTING the cash they already spend on financial services they don't need. Financially savvy people buy only the financial products and services they really need. We have shown you how they do it in each of theinsidersguides.com.

Our members have found that they can save up to $3,000 per year using our Insider's Guides. You can't afford to waste that extra $3,000. You can then buy assets that "grow by themselves." Some members put their money in their own business or the stocks of businesses that pay them earnings. That $3,000 becomes $3,202, then $6,811, then $10,877, until they have $1,000,000. This is your **Wealth Reserve**™.

It is NOT too late

Since you will probably live to be over 90 years of age, you will need your **Wealth Reserve**™ for income or health or custodial care. It is not ridiculous to follow our Insider's advice even at age 60. Our members enjoy buying assets that grow without the need to work more hours. They make sure that the $3,000 they saved goes automatically to their business or the accounts they own. When they work for someone else, members enroll in their employer's retirement plan and some receive a matching amount FREE. If not, they start a **Wealth Reserve**™ §408 trust.

Some ask, where does the $250 a month ($3,000 a year) come from? It comes from learning about the financial products you really need and buying them directly from quality providers. You may NOT be the spouse responsible for buying insurance and investments. You will probably be the spouse who benefits most by investing the savings in a **Wealth Reserve**™ stock mutual fund.

Many members have moved their mutual funds from Fidelity to Vanguard and saved over $3,000 a year. They were paying over 1.2% of their account values *each year* for many years. Now they pay less than 0.20%. Their retirement funds will be half a million dollars greater because they pay 0.2% instead of 1.2% per year until retirement. Compare your present mutual fund to a low-cost leader to see how much you are wasting:
https://personal.vanguard.com/us/faces/JSP/Funds/Compare/CompareEntryContent.jsp?type=etf

Build your **Wealth Reserve**™

Your **Wealth Reserve**™ consists of all the assets your family owns that "grow by themselves." For your family, that may mean retirement plans, home, rental real estate, securities and mutual funds, and a business, if you own one. Female home ownership is at an all-time high with one-fifth of residential real estate now being held by single females. Women are now the primary breadwinners in roughly one-third of U.S. households.

Financially independent people are independent because they use their income to buy more "assets that grow by themselves." Typically their **Wealth Reserve**™ allows them to feel comfortable because they spend less than they make. If their income were to vanish for five years, they would be able to survive—keeping their family and home intact. Most of our members use their retirement plan for the bulk of their **Wealth Reserve**™. Typically they started investing during their working lives and consistently increased the proportion of their income designated for investments.

Women are more likely to lack a personal pension. Women are more likely to lack the experience to manage the family investments. Women are more likely to inherit assets that they do not know how to grow. Although this situation is changing, it has been my experience that many women need to learn how to control their financial life later than men. Women will have a longer time to make sure their assets will take care of them—producing income far beyond what was originally planned.

Women need to educate themselves NOW about what assets their family owns and why they own them. Families usually own mutual funds, securities and rental real estate in various taxable, tax-deferred and tax-FREE accounts. Some have left employers with retirement plans after years of accumulation. Most of them have opened IRA rollover accounts and had the new trustee move the money so they continue compounding without receiving it and paying tax. Women need to understand how TAX-FREE or tax-deferred compounding works so they can control the supply of income after their spouse passes on.

Many families have mutual fund accounts at five or more different firms. Some members, especially women, have seen their **Wealth Reserve**™s grow dramatically over the years because they don't buy and sell funds. Some members invest 10% of their income. Most members with sizable accounts started investing early. They saved for their first home down payment, college funds, vacations and cars. Women need to ensure their family has earmarked long-term funding for *their own* future financial needs. Increase the amount invested by using our Insider's Guides to cut the commissions and fees on their financial service needs.

How your **Wealth Reserve**™ saves you up to 40%

Financially savvy members have used our Insider's Guide to Vehicle Insurance to help them save up to $6,000 over 10 years, for instance. Our Insider explains what you need and don't need and why to keep the deductible high. If you are a safe experienced driver, you can benefit by switching to certain insurers. One of them has been rated No. 1 in customer satisfaction for many years by JD Power and pays YOU dividends. Why pay extra high commissions and subsidize other people's poor driving habits?

Not every member can qualify for every category of savings we explain. However, our Insider provides enough "tricks of the trade" to help almost every member save hundreds of dollars. Members use a **Wealth Reserve**™ Roth IRA to shield their earnings from any taxation. The goal is to have an extra $125,000 tax-FREE when the spouse retires to cover the couple's long-term care needs later on, if any. 13% of women need on-going care.

Another member from Montclair, NJ used our Insider's Guide to Homeowners Insurance to save $5,000 over 10 years. We explain what you need and don't need and why to keep the deductible high and when **NOT to call your agent or insurer.** We show you where to buy if you have a home "at high risk." If you have never had a claim, you may benefit by switching to a "direct writer." Why subsidize others' claims? In some states, you can save 100% or more by using our Insider's hints.

Another member in Vermont dropped his life insurance after realizing that his adult children did not need the protection any more. Further, after consulting our Insider's Guide to Retirement Spending he determined to invest aggressively to insure that he would have enough to retire when he wanted to. He used our Insider's Guide to Buying Mutual Funds and Securities to save 1% a year on his choice of mutual funds and brokerage firms.

Both members are increasing their **Wealth Reserve**™ with money they did not need to spend on insurance. Members use our Insider's Guide to Vehicle Purchases and will save about $10,000 on their choice of cars. Building your **Wealth Reserve**™ protects you against giving money away to banks, especially the $3,000 to $4,000 in interest most people pay every year on credit cards and[1] car loans.

Making your money work for 20 years in your **Wealth Reserve**™ can provide about $51,000, enough for a home down payment, car or education. You will have paid only $30,000 ($3,000 for 10 years) for that $51,000. You borrow from your "bank" to pay cash.

You don't have to make a budget or "tighten your belt."

The **Wealth Reserve**™ strategy works because you don't have to *find* NEW money to build your **Wealth Reserve**™. You use the money you already spend for financial services that you decide you don't need. Instead of buying a car or appliance and paying up to 5 times the price by financing it, you pay cash. However, the cash from your **Wealth Reserve**™ is special. It is "compounded" cash. The $51,000 described above cost you only $30,000! You pay less because you planned ahead. See our Insider's Guide to Banking to avoid paying 5 times the price for large items.

WARNING: This Guide offers a strategy to self-fund your financial needs. This Guide shows you how to drop services you may not need. However, before you change your current accounts, make certain that the alternative plan is in place. Do not close the old account until you have tried the services from your new providers and started your **Wealth Reserve**™.

Typically members are "buy-and-hold" investors. This is what makes women better investors than men. Women are more patient. They know they can't time the market by buying the hot stock or fund. That activity only benefits the brokers and leaves the average investor earning **3.79%** vs 11% according to a DALBARinc.com. Some members use Modern Portfolio Theory (riskglossary.com/) to increase returns as they reduce risk. Women members illustrate this strategy in Chapter 2.

Some members have chosen low-cost index funds to keep their **Wealth Reserve**™-building simple. These members believe that broad market indexes provide their best chance of accumulating at 10-12% annually over the long haul. They don't consider themselves risk-takers but are comfortable leaving 100% of their long-term money in stock funds. Their short-term goals are accomplished by funding low-cost bond/balanced funds. They used Morningstar.com to screen for the funds they use.

How your **Wealth Reserve**™ works

We provided an example of how a **Wealth Reserve**™ works over a lifetime in Chapter 1. Fred and Susan started creating a fund many years ago. They started out just saving for their daughter's college expenses when they got married. They kept using their college fund for more than just college. They used it like a **Wealth Reserve**™ to self-insure and self-fund their lifetime needs. Susan is the investor.

Here are the highlights of the story in which Susan managed her family's financial life.

Fred and Susan had a baby—Natalie—about 35 years ago. They

lived in lower Manhattan. Susan worked with one of our Insiders. Susan asked what to do with the money they received from relatives and friends for Natalie's birth. They wanted to protect their new child's future and to have college money. Both Fred and Susan had good insurance benefits at work. Fred and Susan were already aware of the benefits of investing in the pension where the company matched their contributions—like FREE money—and Uncle Sam waits for his.

Fred and Susan picked the stocks with the highest yield and the lowest price. Susan was an underwriter and knew stock values. They agreed on buying stocks because they could buy them directly from the companies and hold them without paying tax on the increased value until they needed the money. Dividends were reinvested and the income tax was not outrageous.

They had $5,000 from gifts and they contributed $6 a day ($350 monthly). By the time Natalie was 18, Fred and Susan had about $300,000. They were temped to stop investing during the 1978 recession, but Susan kept them on track.

They had a car accident and sold stock to pay for the insurance policy deductible. They were saving about $200 a year by taking the $1,000 deductible.

They wanted a house. The cost of the down payment—$15,000—came from Natalie's college fund. They found that most of the $15,000 withdrawal was money they had already paid tax on. They paid the capital gains tax of 20% on about $5,000 of the $15,000. They avoided the mortgage insurance that because they had a 20% down payment.

They saved on their homeowner's by picking a $5,000 deductible. They saved on credit life, disability, unemployment, and PMI insurance that the mortgage bank tried to add on to their mortgage. All these helped pay for the college fund. For $210 a year, Susan and Fred would have $1,000,000 coverage in case they were sued and needed to pay a lawyer to defend themselves.

They were finally ready for Natalie to go to college. They had $300,000 available for her when she was 18 years old. During this time educational loans were very cheap. So Fred and Susan decided to let the college fund grow—20% to 25% a year—during the 90's. They knew this was unusual because the average gain for Dow stocks was 12% a year. They let the loans grow for the first two years until they could see that they had earned $60,000 for two years straight. So they sold enough stock to pay the loans and the tax of 20% on the stock earnings. Now they realized they did not have to worry about the college loans any more."

Susan told our Insider that they had easily taken care of Natalie's college expense each year from the college fund. They stopped paying for term life insurance policies that she and Fred owned. This saved them another $2,500 a year and they continued to invest the $350 per month.

Susan was disabled within the year. She no longer had disability insurance from work. She was not able to work at all. They decided to cut back on their entertainment, vacation, and hobbies in order to get by on Fred's salary. They also had an emergency expense. They had to sell stock to pay $10,000 for a parent's home repair. The tax on the earnings of the stocks did not push them into the next tax bracket, so they are actually paying much less tax this year anyway. Susan got better and was able to give Natalie a fabulous graduation party and trip to California as a present.

The next year after Natalie graduated; Susan and Fred decided to start their own business. Fred would work part-time. **Susan would work full-time in what she loved**—framing people's pictures. Fred would do the woodwork. Susan would run the store in a charming village nearby. The college fund—now $600,000 or so—gave them the feeling that they would have incomes until they got the store into the black. They didn't need much to pay the store's rent and utilities. The store liability policy was not too bad after Susan picked a higher deductible. Fred's job would provide the health insurance they needed.

The store business allows Fred and Susan to deduct many of the normal expenses associated with their activities. The 'college' fund, no longer for college, allows them to save more on the protection they need for retirement.

They attended a seminar on **long term care insurance** and decided that they can afford it but don't need it. According to page 6 of the Shopper's Guide they received at the seminar, the chance of Fred needing expensive care is 4%; **Susan 13%.** [See our Insider's Guide to Long-term Care Insurance.] If they spent $4,000 a year for up to 30 years, they may never get to use that $120,000 ($2,000 each, times 30 yrs.) because they both are in good health. Anyway, 25% of LTC buyers drop it within two years.

Fred and Susan put the $4,000 in their tax-advantaged retirement plan, connected with their business. This will add another $600,000 for any emergency, including remodeling their home for easy access and hiring a home health aide. These are the most common needs people have, according to the booklet. Worst case, they have assets in a business which helps them with health care.

Fred was still a teacher working part-time and Susan loves the way a picture looks—even bad ones—in a frame.

Lifestyle Protection

A **Wealth Reserve**™ is usually started when people get motivated to save and invest, usually when they have a child. Every one of our members wishes they had started their **Wealth Reserve**™ or 'self-insurance funds' earlier than they did.

The Reserve Fred and Susan have built up is the *real* **meaning of insurance**: it's <u>lifestyle protection</u>. It is easier to create a **Wealth Reserve**™ or 'Self-Insurance Fund' because the Roth IRA or Roth 401k allows most people to use market securities for their important needs without paying any federal tax on the earnings--*ever*. The **Wealth Reserve**™ Roth IRA lets you pay for college, home, health, and disabilities without any federal income tax or penalty. Today, members would be able to supplement their pensions with the $900,000 or so they have accumulated without any federal income taxes—Zero, Nothing, FREE.

No matter what your age, a **Wealth Reserve**™ can be created and used because we are all living longer. No person in retirement has ever told me that they have enough. Investing $250 monthly, $3,000 a year, your Reserve can grow to $300,000 to protect your lifestyle in retirement. You can find the $3,000 a year from savings you experience using our Insider's trade secrets. Search each financial product/service you own to squeeze out the money from charges you don't need.

For a woman, a **Wealth Reserve**™ is the security she needs after everyone else in the family has been taken care of. Creating a new life after the loss of your spouse is a whole lot easier when you have a **Wealth Reserve**™.

Learning to control your family's spending is something you both have to come to together. Learning how to invest over time is easy using the plan we have shown you. These are the two skills you need to ensure your financial health. When your family is no longer around, you will have to manage your financial life yourself. Even if you hire someone else, you better know what they are doing or you won't have your wealth very long.

It is not as difficult as it seems. You may remember when you first starting using a computer or smart phone. There were too many features to grasp all at once but you eventually got it. Now you can't imagine being without your machine. You can learn to manage wealth but it takes time—time to accumulate it and to control it. Our network can support you in your practice.

You can do it because others just like you have done it!

13

The Insider's Guide to a Spending Plan: Who else will build wealth for you?

✓ Grow $1 million from $9 a day
✓ Pay up to 40% less for financial products
✓ Achieve all your goals with what you earn *now*

Your Spending Plan

It is impossible to grow and maintain wealth without a plan of how you spend money. I have seen people receive a large lump sum settlement and blow it all in less than 5 years. Yes, they had a great time, but all the money that could have kept them wealthy for life is gone. Many athletes and lottery winners are bankrupt within 5 years of receiving enough to retire as nobility.

In order to accomplish every one of your goals, you need to construct a spending plan. Otherwise you won't be able to maintain the strategy of accumulating the savings you gain. During our working lives, we earn about $1.5 to $2.5 million before taxes. We can accumulate another $1 million to accomplish all that we want to do in life by using just 10 percent of that income to buy assets that "grow by themselves." The 10 percent can come from money you now waste on financial services you don't need. Investing the 10 percent automatically guarantees the accomplishment of your goals.

Using a Spending Plan is **like brushing your teeth**—it's a habit that isn't that difficult to learn. Then it is automatic. You start your Spending Plan TODAY. Your assets can grow to $1 million or more using compounding—the "most powerful force in the universe" according to Albert Einstein brainyquote.com/quotes/quotes/m/mignonmcla158995.html. This is the secret that the rich use to become richer. You can double the value of your assets every 7-9 years. $9 per day, $250 a month becomes $1 million in 33-37 years; $500 a month becomes $1 mil in 25 years and then $2 million in 31 years.

Every successful independent person has a plan

The **factor** that makes assets "grow by themselves" is earnings compounding over TIME. The seed money comes from commissions and fees you are already paying. Our members have found that they are paying at least $3,000 a year for services they don't need or can buy for less money. TheInsidersGuides show you how and where to buy top-quality financial services for less so that you can redirect that $3,000 FROM your broker, banker, and agent TO your own **Wealth Reserve**™. By putting your plan on automatic, you can unleash the power of compounding. It is TIME not investment advice or skill that can make you financially independent and wealthy.

How assets build your **Wealth Reserve**™

Monthly	Accumulation at 12% per year									
	5	10	15	20	25	30	35	40	45	50
$100	$8,167	$23,004	$49,958	$98,925	$187,884	$349,496	$643,095	$1,176,477	$2,145,469	$3,905,834
$200	$16,334	$46,008	$99,916	$197,850	$375,768	$698,992	$1,286,190	$2,352,954	$4,290,938	$7,811,668
$300	$24,501	$69,012	$149,874	$296,775	$563,652	$1,048,488	$1,929,285	$3,529,431	$6,436,408	$11,717,502
$500	$40,835	$115,020	$249,790	$494,625	$939,420	$1,747,480	$3,215,475	$5,882,385	$10,727,340	$19,529,169

Three Steps to your Spending Plan

You can establish your Spending Plan in three steps. Earn a guaranteed 15% to 29% on your money—PAY OFF credit card debt in the order of the LOWEST balance first. Every extra 25% of the "minimum" payment you pay monthly *slashes* the total amount you will have to pay by 50%.

Begin by just listing all credit card debt balances with the finance charge. Wouldn't it be great to earn that same 15% to 29% on your money that you now give to your banker? You can earn these same rates of return by paying each balance off, one at a time. You can earn a guaranteed 15-30% on your money NOW!

First, pay double or triple the minimum amount on the lowest balance account each month until it's done. Cut that card; don't cancel the account. That lowers your credit score. Do the same for the rest of your cards.

Second, celebrate! You are half-way there.

Third, open a **Wealth Reserve**™ account with the interest you *used* to pay on your cards. One of the low-cost mutual funds allows you to begin with only $100 a month. That is only $3.34 a day—a 'Starbie's. Members illustrated this strategy in Chapter 2. You will have the best tax shelter in America. And it's legal!

You are on your way! As you pay off each card, celebrate by increasing the amount you have automatically invested in your mutual fund by the monthly payments you used to pay. You are buying *your* future, NOT your banker's. Your target is $250 a month. It is automatic, so you never miss the $250. In time, you will have $250,000, then $1,000,000.

Make it simple

Your Spending Plan should be simple. Members find simple plans last longer than the complicated ones. Your Plan consists of all the goals you have decided you want to accomplish in your life as of TODAY. The Plan includes the strategy you plan to use to achieve each goal.

For instance, one Network member wished to buy a luxury car. If she borrowed the $44,100, she would pay $750 for 5 years. She knew that cars lost value very fast. In 5 years, when she finished paying for it, her car would be worth only $25,000 or less. Instead, she learned to use the compounding calculator at moneychimp.com/calculator/compound_interest_calculator.htm to determine that she could invest $500 (not $750) a month for 36 months and buy a three-year old model of the same car for cash. She chose to buy a used Acura TL. See our The Insider's Guide to Vehicle Purchases for details.

Because she didn't buy a new car with credit, she saved $250 a month. Like all of us, she had other goals: she wanted to start her own business.
So instead of spending $750 a month on a car for 5 years, she put $500 a month in her **Wealth Reserve**™ for a luxury car AND $250 a month for her business startup costs. In three years she had completed one goal AND she was on her way to completing her second goal. She spent the same amount—$750 per month for 5 years. She ended up with a luxury car, plus $34,000 without taxes. In five years, this savvy saver had worked her Spending Plan to

achieve TWO of her financial goals for the price of one!!

She says she will keep building her **Wealth Reserve**™. Over TIME, she will be able to achieve any goal. In five to seven years, she will have $123,632 to enhance her business or achieve one of her other goals.

If you buy "assets that grow by themselves," you can help insure yourself and help finance yourself instead of giving your hard-won income to your broker, banker or agent. Your **Wealth Reserve**™ allows you to provide for your own permanent life insurance, long-term care insurance, disability insurance as well as saving up to 40% on other financial products.

Your **Wealth Reserve**™ provides cash for college and retirement funding. It can even pay for luxury cars, vacation homes and your own business start-up at a discount. She paid $750 a month for 10 years ($90,000) and got $123,632 plus her luxury car.

Your **Wealth Reserve**™ allows you to be financially independent like many of our members. Remember, it is TIME not investment skill that creates wealth.

"We continue to make more money when snoring than when active."
Warren Buffet", berkshirehathaway.com/letters/1996

Financially independent people buy only the financial products and services they really need. We have shown you how they do it in each of TheInsidersGuides: banking, mortgage, mutual funds, securities, annuity, life insurance, health insurance, long term care insurance, vehicle insurance, home insurance, lawsuit insurance, vehicle purchases . . . almost any product or service.

Your Spending Plan provides the details of how to use the $3,000 per year saved by using our Insider's Guides. Smart spenders buy "assets that grow by themselves" They put their money in their own business or the stocks of businesses that pay them earnings. That $3,000 becomes $6,811, then $10,877, until they have $1,000,000 in 33 years; $2 mil in 40 years.

Financially independent people have fun with their money. They enjoy buying "assets that grow" without the need to work more hours. They stop wasting their paychecks by making sure that the $3,000 they saved goes automatically to their business, properties or the securities they own. They enjoy it so much that they find a way to save another $3,000 or $250 a month. If they work for someone else, some independents enroll in their employer's retirement plan. Some receive a matching amount for their account FREE. They use a **Wealth Reserve**™ if no match.

Your Spending Plan consists of **real detailed plans**, not vague wishes like playing the lotto in order to become wealthy. You have to be clear about your goals and your spending habits. For instance, most of our members say they want to accumulate $1,000,000 for additional income and medical expenses. For one family, that means identifying exactly where the MONEY will come from and the TIME it will take to get there. You saw an example with the King family above.

Many members have moved their mutual funds to Vanguard and saved over $3,000 a year. Their retirement funds will be half a million greater because they pay 0.2% instead of 1.2% per year until retirement. Your mutual fund accounts contain the greatest opportunity to save.

How to design a Spending Plan

Your Spending Plan consists of all the details of what you want to accomplish and how you will pay for them. Our members accomplish what they *really* want to get done. They do so because they are specific about their goals and specific about how much it will cost and how they will pay for it.

You probably won't be motivated to actually create a Plan until you write down what you want to do. Many people just talk ebri.org/pdf/briefspdf/EBRI_IB_04-20061.pdf. Our members who actually get it done are the ones who dreamed and then wrote down the goal with their spouse and family.

You have to write goals down so that everyone who contributes to making your life and your family happy also makes a formal agreement to prioritize their needs and wants. In other words, to finish this goal you have to decide it comes first or before other 'wants.' If your spouse gets all excited about buying the new whatever they saw on TV, it is hard to say "no." If you want to buy yourself that new *whatever* at the mall, you can't say "yes." You both must agree on the priority of goals.

Before credit cards, it was easier to wait and save. Now it is too easy to give in. So we sink deeper in debt—usually for stuff we can do without after the thrill is gone.

A Spending Plan helps to build consensus in the family. It provides a guide to getting all that we want. We just have to put our goals on the list of priorities. We don't have to say "no" to ourselves and our family. You just put it on the list to get done. You pay for your future first before other distractions destroy it.

Your Spending Plan is this list. Put all goals that cost money in order of priority. This list usually includes anything that is usually financed or charged to a credit card that takes more than a month to pay off.

The items we have seen on lists are the annual vacation, a vacation home down payment, a boat, a diamond necklace, summer camp, a start-up business fund, college fund, retirement fund to supplement a pension, a retirement fund without a pension, a health-care fund, luxury car, foreign travel, a family legacy, and a foundation to carry on a family activity. See the King family's list below.

You need to make your list now. You don't need to fear that your list is not complete. Our list changes all the time. Some things get pushed down or off the list, others added. Without a list, you fool yourself. Allstate's 2006 Retirement Reality Check survey shows that 70 percent of Americans polled–regardless of age, gender, household income and education–describe themselves as "financially independent." But, despite such optimism, 40 percent of respondents admit they are not saving seriously for retirement. They could not survive for 5 years if they had no income. **YOU can't be independent without a plan**.

Our members say they review their list of goals about once a quarter when they receive their brokerage and mutual fund statements. You will need to add a cost to each goal. If it is not clear what amount to use because the goal is unclear or is far off in TIME, you need to do some research. See the steps in Chapter 2.

How long will each goal take? Use this calculator moneychimp.com/calculator/compound_interest_calculator.htm to give you an estimate of what you can accumulate in time. For retirement, the average retiree today has a nest egg of about $200,000 but relies on a pension for 30% and Social Security for 44% of their income, according to ***MONEY***, April 2005. You may need a nest egg of $500,000 or more if your company offers no paid retirement plan and Social Security benefits are cut. You need to create a **Wealth Reserve**™ to make sure you have enough for your goals on the list and the unexpected.

Most people don't set up detailed plans, so they end up with less. One survey said 52% of Americans don't know how much they need to live on. 36% have not saved for retirement. 57 % have a retirement account BUT the median (half below, half above) amount held is only $2,000. A few wealthy people push the average to $50,000. Most owe more than they own. Indebtedness is a national addiction. The average debt, per household, NOT counting mortgage debt, is about $14,500. Total personal debt is $84,454. aarp.org, bls.gov, banking.senate.gov, bankrate.com.

Rely on your **Wealth Reserve**™

Your **Wealth Reserve**™ consists of all the assets you own that "grow by themselves." Your **Wealth Reserve**™ can provide you with the extra money to reach all your goals, in time. However, without a plan, a **Wealth Reserve**™ will never have time to grow and earn interest for you. Most people just spend like there is no tomorrow.

Financially independent people are independent because they use their income to buy more assets that "grow by themselves." Typically their **Wealth Reserve**™ allows them to feel comfortable because they spend less than they make. If their income were to be cut for five or more years, they would be able to survive—keeping their family and home intact. They don't borrow money except to earn more than the cost of the loan. Usually a home mortgage or business loan is all they owe.

Your Spending Plan assures you that your income will be multiplied by compounding to make it possible to reach every goal you set for yourself. TIME and the 10% of income you invest is the ***only way*** to spend $4,000,000 on earned income of $2,000,000 during your whole lifetime.

Saved $120,000

Mr.and Mrs. K., in their 60's, compared LTC with a joint annuity that had a LTC waiver for their needs. The annual cost was $2,000 each for a LTC policy. $50,000 annuity costs 2.5% annually but taxes must be paid by heirs if not used for LTC. Wealth Reserve is tax-friendly now and heirs pay no tax on accumulation of $1/2 million if not used.

Divide your List

Consider your goals. Separate the short-term goals from the long-term goals like the King's. For each goal and its cost to be accomplished, find the amount you need to invest. For goals with large amounts like a $1,000,000 retirement fund, you need to invest in the stock market for 38 years at $250 a month. You can do this in an employer plan, a Roth or regular IRA or a taxable account, in preferred order. A Roth 401k or IRA means no tax on withdrawals. Members use low-cost mutual funds. You have a 86% chance of earning 10%-12% a year with index funds.

For goals with smaller amounts to be done in less than 5 years, you can estimate the growth of your **Wealth Reserve**™ using the MoneyChimp calculator at moneychimp.com/calculator/compound_interest_calculator.htm to estimate the numbers. We use 6%-8% compounded 12 times a year for separate goals less than 5 years. If you have been investing for some time, you can 'borrow' $10,000 for a vacation and repay yourself in 3 years. If you just started to invest, you will need to double your contributions. If you try to hurry the process along by moving in and out of hot mutual funds, it may take longer. Our Insider's Guide to Buying Mutual Funds and Securities shows why it is TIME, not investment prowess, which wins for you. Our Insider explains when to invest inside a tax-favored or taxable account.

If most of your goals will take over 5 years to complete and you are more comfortable using mutual funds of different types of assets (see Modern Portfolio Theory in Chapter 2), you can accumulate enough money in your **Wealth Reserve**™ to fund any short-term goal you like with less chance of loss. For instance, our member who bought her luxury car with her **Wealth Reserve**™ had a considerable balance in her account already. She was able to take advantage of the fact that the stock market funds rose 29% in 2003 and 11% in 2004. She had the guts to continue to invest $750 a month during the 2001 and 2002 market downturns (stock on sale).

Your Spending Plan should include your goals, their costs and how much per month you are paying in order for your future to come true.

Member Bill's list is an example: **Bill of Pennsylvania**

Education for our son	18 years $90,000	$100 month
Expand own business	20 years $100,000	$100 month
Retire with 80% of current income	39 years $1,000,000	$100 month

WHERE DID BILL GET THE EXTRA $300/month TO INVEST?

How your **Wealth Reserve**™ saves up to 40% on financial products

Financially savvy members have used our Insider's Guides to save. For example, Bill used the Insider's Guide to Vehicle Insurance to help him save up to $6,000 over 10 years. He saved $200/month on his 401k choices. Another member from Colorado used our Insider's Guide to Homeowners Insurance to save $5,000 over 10 years. Another member in California dropped his life insurance after realizing that his adult kids did not need the protection any more.

Building your **Wealth Reserve**™ protects you against giving money away to banks, especially the $2,000 to $3,000 in interest most people pay every year on credit cards and car loans.

Making your money work for 10 years in your **Wealth Reserve**™ can provide about $50,000, enough for a home down payment, car, vacation, etc. You will have paid only $30,000 ($3,000 for 10 years) for that $50,000. You borrow from your "bank" to pay cash.

You don't have to make a budget or "tighten your belt."

Make your money work for you, not you work for your money. The **Wealth Reserve**™ strategy works because you don't have to *find* the money to build your **Wealth Reserve**™. You use the money you already spend for financial services that you decide you don't need. Instead of buying a car or appliance and paying up to 5 times the price with finance charges, you pay cash. Remember, the cash from your **Wealth Reserve**™ is special—the $50,000 described above cost you only $30,000!. You pay less because you planned ahead.

WARNING: This Guide offers advice on how to self-fund your needs. This Guide shows you how to drop services you may not need. However, before you change your current accounts, make certain that the alternative plan is in place. Do not close the old account until you have tried the services from your new providers and started your **Wealth Reserve**™.

I repeat: Savvy investors do not try to time the market by buying the hot stock or fund. You are going to experience the strong emotions of greed and fear. When you earn 20% or more in one year, you will feel rich and want to spend more. When you lose money, you will want to sell all. At those times, go back to the chart of Dr Harvey. The lines go up and down—find where you are on the line and look ahead. The line comes back to the average of 10-12%. If you sell or spend your assets, you will end up with 3.79% like everyone else. "Stay the course," as Vanguard founder John Bogle advises.

How your Spending Plan might work

Refer back to the example of Fred and Susan. Think of how their Spending Plan worked over their lifetime. Fred and Susan started out just saving for their daughter's college expenses when she was born. They kept using their college fund for more than just college. They used it as a **Wealth Reserve**™ to self-insure and self-fund their lifetime needs. It allowed them to pay for things they planned and did not anticipate. They started their own business later because they had the money to do it even though they didn't plan it that way.   Recall the important events:

➔ Fred and Susan had a baby and started to **buy stocks on a monthly basis** in order to have a college fund. They had a goal and a time frame in mind. They stuck with it.

➔ They had a car accident and had to tap their **Wealth Reserve**™ for the **$1,000 deductible**. However, they had been saving about $200 a year on their car insurance. That's $3,600 saved over 18 years.

➔ The cost of their **house down payment**—$15,000—came from

Natalie's college fund. They paid less tax on the earnings than if they had saved the amount in a CD. They avoided PMI insurance by paying 20% down. That saved them another 18,000 over 20 years.

➔ They saved on their homeowner's insurance by picking a **$5,000 deductible**.

➔ They had over $300,000 available for her when Natalie was 18 years old. She chose a very good **state school that cost less** than $10,000 a year.

➔ Fred and Susan decided to let the college fund grow—20% to 25% a year—during the 90's. When they were ready, they sold **enough stock to pay the loans** and the tax of 20% on the stock earnings.

➔ They **stopped** paying for **life insurance** policies that she and Fred owned. This saved them another $2,500 a year and they continued to invest the $350 per month.

➔ Susan was disabled within the year but they **cut expenses** instead of having disability insurance. Fred's income was part of their disability plan.

➔ They had to sell stock to pay $10,000 for a **parent's home repair**. They didn't own a service contract. They paid 20% tax on the gains. They saved the interest on a home loan and service fees.

➔ Susan and Fred decided to **start their own business**. The college fund—now $600,000 or so—gave them the feeling that they would have incomes until they got the store into the black. They didn't need much to pay the store's rent and utilities. The store liability policy was not too bad after Susan picked a higher deductible. Fred's job would provide the health insurance they needed.

➔ The business allows Fred and Susan to deduct many of the normal expenses associated with their activities. There are few extra taxes on the additional benefits.

➔ They attended a seminar on **long-term care insurance** and decided that they can afford it but don't need it. They figured that if they spent $4,000 a year for up to 30 years, they may never get to use that $120,000 ($2,000 each, times 30 yrs) because they both are in good health.

➔ They had about $1.2 million in their fund in 1999.

A Spending Plan is usually started when people have a goal. Usually young people get motivated to save and invest when they get married or buy a house. Every one of our members wishes they had started their **Wealth Reserve**™ earlier than they did. However, because we are living longer, there is enough time for many goals.

The Reserve Fred and Susan have built up is the real meaning of insurance: it is **lifestyle protection**. Today it is even easier to create a **Wealth Reserve**™ because the Roth IRA allows most working people to use market securities for their important needs without paying any tax* on the earnings, **ever**. Pension plans, 401k and IRAs only delay tax until retirement when you may need the tax you put off paying.

The Roth IRA lets you pay for a home and disabilities without penalty. In the future, you would be able to live on $1,000,000 without any federal or state* income taxes—Zero, Nothing, FREE.

Even if you did not start early, a **Wealth Reserve**™ can still be created and used by most people because we are all living longer. Even late starters can make a **Wealth Reserve**™ of $250,000 tax-FREE to insure their lifestyle in retirement. Your **Wealth Reserve**™ is like the treasury department of your family business. It helps you create financial freedom. You can have anything you want; you just have to avoid giving away the money you earn to financial middle people. It is your Wealth and your Reserve to protect your family from the unexpected.

* As of 2013, most states follow the IRS rules and do not tax qualified distributions (age 59½, death, disability, first-time home buyer). irs.gov/retirement/article/0,,id=137307,00.html

Your Spending Plan should look something like the written statement on the next page. The Insiders Guides can help you find the money for the contributions so you don't have to work more hours or cut out the things you love. See TheInsidersGuids.com for the Guides.

Keep this graph in mind when you plan you spending. Low-cost stock mutual funds are still the best place to keep your money for goals that require large amounts of money over more than 10 years ahead. After 10 years, broad market indexes are consistent.

Your Spending Plan:

Start Today   Saving sources

Goal	Cost	Time	Monthly
____	____	____	____
____	____	____	____
____	____	____	____
____	____	____	____
____	____	____	____
____	____	____	____
____	____	____	____
____	____	____	____

Vehicle insurance
Homeowners
Life insurance
Mutual fund fees
Mortgage PMI
Accident Insurance
Bank fees
Credit card charge
Other fees
Commissions
$4 coffee/beer
$350 car payments
$100 gardener
Club fees
Cell phone bill
Premium cable

Examples of goals:

Goal	Cost	Time	Monthly
Emergency fund	$8,000	5 years	$100
Retirement	$1M	39 years	$100
Luxury used car	$20,000	6 years	$200
Education	$90,000	18 years	$100
Business	$100,000	20 years	$100
Down Payment	$40,000	5 years	$500
Vacation	$2,500	2 years	$100
Remodel home	$65,000	7 years	$500
____	____	____	____
____	____	____	____
____	____	____	____

YOU ARE PREPARED FOR EMERGENCIES

You *will have* money and insurance to handle ALL emergencies. Uncle Sam helps—pay ZERO taxes thanks to your Roth 401k or Roth IRA. You avoid the high costs that can rob you of up to 63% of our account. You buy only the products you need, DIRECTLY.

You can now buy every financial product and service at a discount. You could be saving 40% on your vehicle insurance, 300% on your life insurance, 10% on your homeowner's, 100% on disability, 100% on long term care, 15% on health, 30% on banking, 20% on a mortgage, 30% on educational funds, 200% on mutual funds, 40% on your next car, 20% on an annuity or wealth transfer, and even 10% on business insurance.

Many of us have saved $3,000 on our financial products. With planning, we spend as a savvy independent person. We have all the tools that wealthy people use to get and stay rich. Creating wealth is about **patience**. The hard part is **letting your money work** for you. We learn to let our money compound over time. $9 a day invested in stock funds can be worth $1,000,000 in about 33 years. This one account will provide our borrowing, insurance deductible, retirement income and supplemental health care spending needs.

Use your **Wealth Reserve**™ to cover all your manageable risks. You have the right policy to protect you in emergencies. Our financial industry insiders have shown you the "tricks of the trade" but you have to shop to save on the products and services when you need them. You can now buy the best financial services that they do and **avoid high fees and commissions**. Your savings builds your **Wealth Reserve**™ not theirs. You can control your own financial life and security and that's what most people really want.

You want to be able to do it yourself. You don't want to depend on the industry to build your wealth. They're building their own. You need to build your own $1,000,000* **Wealth Reserve**™. The *Insider's Guides* help you buy the products you need. Don't buy what the salespeople have to sell. Most don't carry the best offers for *your* benefit anyway. They hate the fiduciary rule.

You need to protect your own lifestyle in the 21st century. The industry has changed. You can BUY DIRECTLY now. Buy only the financial services you need. You don't want to waste your money helping salespeople hit their goals. We have provided the unbiased advice to make decisions. Build your confidence and pride in your own way. This is our members' motto:

"Give a man a fish; you have fed him for today.

Teach a man to fish; and you have fed him for a lifetime."

This is the *Simple Financial Life*

Follow our alerts dankeppel.blogspot.com. They help you stay current with savings ideas. Shop for insurance discounts every two years. You can put the ideas into practice if they are relevant to your financial independence. No one knows better than you do what you need. In time, you'll feel you can handle your financial future.

Your **Wealth Reserve**™ compounds to create your independent financial future. Using our simple strategy, your **Wealth Reserve**™ would have grown to provide for all your goals. This is a better way to protect yourself in the future and live the *Simple Financial Life*. amazon.com/Simple-Financial-Life-

And if you have questions, we are available to answer them by email. Just send your questions to me at IANBooksEditor@Yahoo.com. I am available to consult with you by telephone. theinsidersguides.com/services.

The Simple Financial Life

$9 a day is worth $1 million in the future

By age 30:

1. Pick your goals and form a financial strategy in 15 minutes. Our Simple, Easy and Wise Plan is Chapter 2. Your first choice: Set up your **Wealth Reserve**™—$9 a day can become a $1 million using assets that "grow by themselves." Set up automatic investing. Second choice: tax-advantaged retirement plan at work **if they match** contributions. Patience is all that's required.
2. Protect your family and assets using our Insider's Guides so you

buy where financial insiders do. You can self-insure some of your smaller risks like companies do. For instance, once your **Wealth Reserve**™ is started, you can raise the deductibles on your auto and home insurance. You can eliminate other insurance premium payments for non-catastrophic coverage. Instead of the insurer earning 10-12% on your premiums, your Reserve does!

3. Plan your spending wisely. This is the time to establish the habit of spending less than you receive. All financially-independent people mentioned that trait as the one that helped them the most. Use your own Self-Funded 'bank' instead of credit cards or bank loans. Life insurance is NOT an investment. All of our Guides are available at Amazon.com: http://editor570.wix.com/IANbooks

By age 40:

1. Refine your goals and update your financial strategy. If you have not been investing 10% of your income, catch up by investing 15% now. Cutting a few non-essentials now could mean having a **Wealth Reserve**™ of $1,000,000 or more to accomplish all your goals.

Forty-eight percent of employees rank "outliving their savings" as the greatest retirement fear, according to MetLife's Employee Benefits Trend Study. Almost as many (43%) are concerned that during their own retirement they will need to provide for the long-term care needs of others, such as a spouse or relative.   ☐

2. Establish a business to do what you do well, but for your own benefit. Many financially independent people are self-employed. Business owners' net worth average $245,000. The tax system rewards business activity. In the years 1996 through 2000, 61% of corporations did not pay taxes. *USNews* 5/17/4 Legal tax-shelters allow US firms to lease foreign (eg: Dortmund, Germany) city sewers back to their city owners to eliminate their own US taxes. Wachovia Bank alone avoided $3B in taxes that way. *PBS* 2/19/4.

GE got $4.7 BILLION from us as a refund in 2010. *NYDailyNews* 4/13/12. You are three times more likely to be audited as an individual payer than as a business. The IRS found massive fraud at Enron in 1993 but officials let it continue, according to David Johnston, *Perfectly Legal*, p. 174. Business owners and executives enjoy several levels of benefits from their activities, including favorable tax-deferred compensation, wealth accumulation, and personal living accommodation in terms of low-cost loans, vehicles, planes, apartments, and entertainment. See how it's done in *Forbes* 6/21/4 p.140. Also your firm can have US federal grants pay for security: cameras, fencing, and communications equipment. *CBSNews* 5/25/4.

The tax system allows higher income people to pay less as a percent of their income in income tax now than those of moderate means. Congress instituted the AMT in 1967 to insist that the wealthy pay some income tax. However, Congress has not adjusted the AMT for the rich. Now the AMT does the reverse. Your business deductions can reduce taxes. According to the Congressional Budget Office, Report 4, APRIL 15, 2004:

> "Taxpayers with AGI between $100,000 and $500,000 will be hit hardest by the AMT: in 2010, over 90 percent of them will have AMT liability. Much of their income is taxed at 25 percent or less under the regular tax, compared with the 26 percent and 28 percent rates for the AMT." ☐

By age 50:

1. We are living longer. This requires more money to live on during the retirement years. Living to age 100, as many will, requires financial planning that most of us have never had to do. Most professionals agree that a larger portion of assets with a growth rate above inflation will be needed to sustain us for 30 or 40 years. According to a Congressional Budget Office Report, MARCH 18, 2004,

> "...roughly half of boomer households are on track to accumulate enough wealth to maintain their current standard of living if the heads of those households retire when they now plan to. At the other end of the spectrum, perhaps a quarter of the households--many of them low-income households with low-skilled workers--have accumulated very few assets thus far and are likely to find themselves largely dependent on government benefits in retirement. [Others] may face significant shortfalls: if they earn relatively low returns on their savings, retire before age 62, and never choose to draw on their housing equity, they may experience a significant decline in

consumption during retirement."
As a result, households can make up for earlier shortfalls in retirement savings with surprisingly modest changes in behavior."

2. Most of us can make those "modest change in behavior" and use our extra time wisely. By age 50, most people know what they want and can save and invest to obtain their goals. The financial planning retirement target age of 65 is a mistake. This is now the prime age of competency and effectiveness. It is still not too late to accumulate a **Wealth Reserve**™ to make sure you never run out of an income for medical care.

Entrepreneurship may become the vehicle for your new career in areas of service or invention. The cost of health care has risen to the level that may require most people to have some connection to a business just to maintain a reasonable level of health care coverage. For financial planning purposes, establishing an organization to carryout or maintain your activities may be the best move.

3. Most people want to help others. If you want to go beyond writing a check to charity once a year, a foundation that can support your activities is not as expensive as it used to be. Mutual fund companies will do all the paperwork for you, allowing you to make a contribution now, and then spread the giving over the coming years, allowing the money to grow in the interim. All the future growth or income earned on your contribution is tax-FREE. Your gifts are tax-deductible. If you have bigger plans, a nonprofit corporation can provide you with the full array of support services. See our Retirement Spending Plan above.

By age 60:

1. Relive your past/college years. You can now go back to college and live the care-free life again. Study what you really want to. Go on that dig to South America or Africa. Or start a co-op. Live with others on a farm the way you wanted to when you were 25. Or, tour America with your favorite band or drive to every national park while they are still open.

2. Redefine your goals and update your financial strategy. You may live to be 100. That is 40 more years. Maintain stock funds in your portfolio to fight inflation. $1,000,000 can produce $80,000 a

year tax-FREE. You are more likely to run out of money than die.

Grow Your **Wealth Reserve**™!

Using the model of how businesses protect and fund themselves, your **Wealth Reserve**™ is a **self-insurance lifestyle treasury** that grows from the money you save on all the financial services you buy using our *Insider's Guides*. You can save up to $3,000 a year, control your financial services costs and provide protection from many kinds of risks. This method of protection is now possible because of changes in the financial services industry and the example of those who have become financially independent. The **Wealth Reserve**™ is your self-funded "bank" so you avoid using financing which is really compounding in reverse. **You EARN interest;** you do NOT PAY interest. Many people, just like you, have learned to be self-sufficient—accumulating wealth and not having to worry about money. And you pay no income taxes.

Your future is in your hands. Put the *power of compounding* to work for you. As Warren Buffett admitted, ""My wealth has come from a combination of living in America, some lucky genes, and **compound interest**."

Avoid the wealth killers—fees, commissions, charges, loads, AND taxes. Buy value—quality at the right price. Financial products are commodities today. Buy only the benefits you need, not the salesperson's approval. **Shop** like you shop for "groceries, … not perfume," as legendary investor Ben Graham confided.

You never have to say "I don't have the money" again!

Monthly	Accumulation at 12% per year									
	5	10	15	20	25	30	35	40	45	50
$100	$8,167	$23,004	$49,958	$98,925	$187,884	$349,496	$643,095	$1,176,477	$2,145,469	$3,905,834
$200	$16,334	$46,008	$99,916	$197,850	$375,768	$698,992	$1,286,190	$2,352,954	$4,290,938	$7,811,668
$300	$24,501	$69,012	$149,874	$296,775	$563,652	$1,048,488	$1,929,285	$3,529,431	$6,436,408	$11,717,502
$500	$40,835	$115,020	$249,790	$494,625	$939,420	$1,747,480	$3,215,475	$5,882,385	$10,727,346	$19,529,169

*Accumulation over 33 years averaged 11% with $250 a month. The **Wealth Reserve**™ is your tax shelter: a gift from Uncle Sam.

Resources

Compounding
Moneychimp.com/calculator/compound_interest_calculator.htmr
Amateur stock pickers not sellers Aaii.com/
Mutual fund costs Sec.gov/answers/mffees.htm
Mutual fund fees Sec.gov/investor/tools/mfcc/mfcc-int.htm
Mutual fund investing Sec.gov/answers/mutfund.htm
Government studies http://www.cbo.gov/
MF, ETF, Stock information Finance.yahoo.com/
Details on Rothira.com/
Details on Roth 401k Bankrate.com/brm/news/sav/20050518a1.asp
Details on Irahelp.com/
Glossary Investorwords.com/
Greatest investor Buffett's comments: Berkshirehathaway.com/

Theinsidersguides.com   You can save up to . . .

Vehicle Insurance	$6,000 over 10 years
Homeowner's Insurance	$2,000 over 10 years
Life Insurance	$20,000 over 20 years
Lawsuit Insurance	$3,000 over 10 years
Health Insurance	$5,000 over 10 years
Disability Insurance	$5,000 over 10 years
Long Term Care	$40,000 over 20 years
Education Funding	$20,000 over 18 years
Retirement Spending	$1,000s over 30 years
Banking	$3,000 each year
Annuities	$20,000 over 20 years
Mutual Funds/Securities	$3,000 each year
Spending Plan	Reach every goal
Vehicle Purchase	$10,000 per vehicle
Mortgage Purchase	$3,000 per contract
Wealth Reserve™	$1,000,000
Wealth Transfer	$20,000 over 10 years
What NOT to buy	101 products to avoid
Living Insurance	$120,000 over 20 years
Survivors	It is your life now
Self-insurance	$20,000 over 20 years
Self-Funded 'bank"	$125,000 over 15 years
Business	$30,000 over 10 years
Women	It is your life

Learn to invest; not speculate

*The **Millionaire Next Door**: The Surprising Secrets of America's Wealthy*, Thomas Stanley, William Danko
*The **Wealthy Barber***, David Chilton
*Common Sense on Mutual Funds: New Imperatives for the **Intelligent Investor***, John C Bogle
*A **Random Walk** Down Wall Street*, Burton Malkiel.
*Stocks for the Long Run: The Definitive Guide to Financial Market Returns and **Long-Term Investment Strategies***, Jeremy J. Siegel, Donald G. Coxe
Everything You've Heard About Investing is Wrong!, William Gross
***Psychology** and the Stock Market*, David Dreman
*Fooled by **Randomness***, Nassim Teleb
*Against the Gods: The Remarkable **Story of Risk***, Peter L Bernstein
*Winning with Index Mutual Funds: **How to beat Wall Street** at its own game*, Jerry Tweddell & Jack Pierce
*The Only Guide to a **Winning Investment Strategy** You'll Ever Need*, Larry Swedroe
One Up on Wall Street, Peter Lynch
***Ordinary People**, Extraordinary Wealth*, Ric Edelman
*The Intelligent **Investor***, Benjamin Graham, Warren E. Buffett (Preface)
*Eight Steps to **Seven Figures***, Charles B. Carlson
***Bogle** on Mutual Funds*, John C. Bogle
***Earn More** (Sleep Better): The Index Fund Solution*, Richard E. Evans
*Perfectly Legal: The Secret Campaign to **Rig Our Tax System** to Benefit the Super–Rich - and Cheat Everybody Else*, David Cay Johnston
*Maximize **Your IRA***, Neil Downing
*Index Your Way to **Investment Success***, Walter R. Good, Roy W. Hermansen
*Tricks of the Trade: An Insider's Guide to Using a **Stockbroker***, Mark Dempsey
*Mobius on **Emerging Markets***, Mark Mobius
*25 **Myths** You've Got to Avoid-- If You Want to Manage Your Money Right: The New Rules for Financial Success*, Jonathan Clements
Investment Policy: How to Win the Loser's Game, Charles D. Ellis
***Wealth Without Wall Street**: Buy Direct -- Avoid the Commissions, Fees, Loads*, Dan Keppel
*The **Simple Financial Life**: How to get what you want without going into debt and living paycheck to paycheck*, Dan Keppel
***Build Wealth Without Extra Money or Time**: You don't need to budget or get an extra job*, Dan Keppel

Your Unbiased Advisor Network

All of the Insiders' Guides were written with the help of my friends and colleagues. Most are industry professionals who work or have worked in the financial services industry. Many financial services firms have discarded their fiduciary trust role and are targeting you in their "asset-gathering" profit plans. Most firms are focused on consolidating their share of the global market, not on helping you.

We think most advisers believe they are 'unbiased' advisors but most have little choice in which products to sell. Products are chosen by the management based on product profitability. Most salespeople are given ample incentives to push specific products, no matter what they say. *Investmentnews.com* 4/3/9. "Many insurers have set up bogus reinsurance companies and other arrangements that reward top producers who are given equity stakes in these third-party entities," according to an insurer's attorney. "Insurance companies' higher payouts for proprietary products are not as well documented as the use of proprietary funds by the major brokers," a securities attorney admitted. *Investmentnews.com* 3/5/7

We are providing this *less biased* information because we are unhappy with our industry's role in NOT helping to educate their fellow citizens. We are unhappy that there is no basic financial education (beyond balancing your checkbook) in our schools. Consequently, those who need help the most are being left further behind.

The disturbing facts we see:

86% of high school seniors think that the **best** long term growth investment is a **savings** account. (Jump Start 2006)

The top 10% of American earners capture over 40% of the nation's income. First time in 65 years! (*NYTimes* 6/25/6)

The very top 1% took nearly one fourth (23.5%) of all America's income in 2007.

The average inflation-adjusted hourly wage declined by more than 7 percent from 1976 to 2007. extremeinequality.org/

52% of Americans don't know how much they need to live on.

36% have not saved for retirement. 57% have a retirement account BUT the median amount held is only $2,000. (BLS.gov)

Our approach: Learn how to succeed financially!

We believe it is more fun to have financial independence than live paycheck to paycheck. You need to have control over your financial life to be happy. You can't rely on those that sell financial services to give you the best advice for your lifestyle. They can't make a living selling no-load low-fee products. The **Simple Financial Life** puts you in control. You buy only the financial services you need, when you need them, using information from our Insiders to save. You invest this savings in the same way professionals do—a diversified mutual fund that beats 86% of all retail funds. (*BusinessWeek* 4/09) You create your own **Wealth Reserve**™, a self-insuring and self-financing fund that protects your lifestyle, now and later, when you really need it.

We feel that most people would be better off if they used the same low-cost products and services that we professionals do. By using our Insider information about products and services, you can buy the best products and save. Most of the products and companies industry professionals use carry the highest financial ratings. These companies' products are a better value—low cost/high quality—because they are not advertised and do not pay high fees or commissions. In other words, **we usually can't sell them** but we buy them for ourselves. Now you can.

For instance, most mutual funds have high expenses, high commissions and don't provide returns that consistently beat their benchmarks. If you buy mutual funds from a bank, brokerage or inside your employer's 401K plan, you are usually forced to buy the ones which benefit the sellers most.

We believe that the industry makes investing for your goals too complicated and costly. Our members, those who use our Guides, became financially successful by using the "tricks of the trade" provided by our Insiders. Some of our members have provided important experiences that I share with every member in the weekly Alert. Most members have uncovered $3,000 or more per year in wasted fees, premiums, loads, charges, etc by using our Guides. They have invested these savings and are on the way to reaching their goals. Our Insiders provide Email support as they can. I help members by providing unbiased advice.

We don't sell products. Our Insiders are less biased. For instance, would you be better off buying that new improved indexed annuity your banker/broker/agent wants to sell you? Sellers who make their living selling products will never tell you about low-cost annuities or better alternatives. We think you need to know about low-cost alternatives. You need to compare products with the same benefits, just like you do in clothes. For instance, if you decide to buy an annuity, buy the low-cost one directly from the insurer and skip the commission and hidden fees.

I am The Guides' editor. I worked for a Wall Street securities firm and two banks over the last 20 years. I managed sales units. I saw that brokers/agents/bankers sell only the products that were profitable for the firm. It is not in their interest to tell you about better alternatives. They can't sell products with low annual costs, for instance, even if they are the best alternatives for you. That's correct! Brokers can't offer the most popular low-cost mutual funds. Agents can't offer one of the least expensive life insurance plans for most people.

Commoditization in all financial services.

Your accounts and your trust are being bought and sold almost everyday. Banks, insurers and mutual funds are trying to combine in a way that they can control larger pools of your money. These new global competitors trade your accounts to gain world dominance. Bond guru, Bill Gross calls them the "capital market vigilantes." Consequently, most of the financial industry operates for its best interests, not yours. For investors, fund owners have become the **new robber barons**, adding more volume and fees while performance, compared to their benchmarks, continues to fall. We believe you do not need to be mistreated anymore. There is a better way!

To succeed, independent people have to learn to take advantage of better information and access to the products and services of independent companies. We believe in the advice Benjamin Graham, legendary investor, gave to investors: buy financial products like you buy "groceries, **not perfume**." Buy value. Understand what you are getting for your money. You can obtain quality products at low cost by seeking out providers who focus their attention on you—the customer—instead of their sales force. Every financially-independent person learned by questioning what they receive for their money. Most learned the hard way that you must understand the VALUE of what you buy, not just their TV commercial. We want to encourage this attitude by helping you discover these "customer-centered" financial services providers. We are your coaches.

"Customer-centered" mutual funds, brokers, bankers, insurers, and lenders have learned to listen to you—the customer—not industry hype. We think they will be the firms that will be responsive to you now and in the future when you need them. Customer-centered firms are well-established and 'young-at-heart' even though they are just as old and financially strong as the companies you've heard about. The difference is they don't make you pay for their million-dollar salesmen, sales contests, kick-backs, rebates, and expensive advertising. They pass these savings on to you.

Customer-centered manufacturers have found ways to give customers what they want, when they want it, the way they want it. The 21st century way to buy is to buy DIRECT: Like Dell.com, customer-focused providers offer individuals a "custom-built" program, directly, at lower cost. Even complicated buys, like diamonds, can be accomplished this way. BlueNile.com lets you "build your own engagement ring," and buy DIRECT. A financial product is not any more sophisticated than a computer or expensive as a diamond. Consider how discount brokerage firms have made it easy for anyone to research, buy and manage their stocks, bonds and funds. Our members have learned to buy banking, insurance, mortgages, credit, and almost every product in the same way. All the companies that Network members use are top quality with high ratings, like USAA, TIAA, Vanguard, SBLI, and Amica.

It is our goal that you will buy only the products and services you need and use the savings to invest for the future. Our wish for you is to become financially independent like Susan and Fred, and now their daughter Natalie. I formed our Network to help working people find the best way to reach their goals. The current industry business models are broken. We can do it ourselves with a little help. No one knows our dreams better than we do.

Your ideas and suggestions are important to all of us as Network members: Email me at editor@TheInsiderSGuides.com.

Start today! No one else can do it for you!

Call Vanguard or TIAA right now. Set up automatic contributions right out of your checking account. "I never miss the money since I don't see it," as one of my clients says.

Expect the market to go down. Don't panic. Review the chart on page 39. Stocks are the only way to accumulate $1,000,000.

Remember the crash of 1987. Those who sold after the drop of 23% were left with a loss. Those who held on had positive returns for the year and their accounts returned to the August 1987 highs within two years.

Don't sell and buy back securities. There were only 40 days from 1950 to 2007 that produced 70% of all the S&P 500 index's total returns. That is only 2% of the time or <u>40 out of 14,528</u>. You will lose money if you trade! John Bogle, *Don't Count on It*, p 169. Now relax and enjoy **The Simple Financial Life!**

The secret to building wealth: PATIENCE—Let compounding work. "The stock market is simply the transfer of wealth from the **impatient to the patient**", says Warren Buffett, world's greatest investor. Buy and hold low-cost stock mutual funds automatically by having your Roth IRA trustee debit your account monthly for the same amount. Try to reach 10% of your income as quickly as possible. Do nothing else.

Prominently display this chart on your refrigerator and desk.

Monthly	Accumulation at 12% per year									
	5	10	15	20	25	30	35	40	45	50
$100	$8,167	$23,004	$49,958	$98,925	$187,884	$349,496	$643,095	$1,176,477	$2,145,469	$3,905,834
$200	$16,334	$46,008	$99,916	$197,850	$375,768	$698,992	$1,286,190	$2,352,954	$4,290,938	$7,811,668
$300	$24,501	$69,012	$149,874	$296,775	$563,652	$1,048,488	$1,929,285	$3,529,431	$6,436,408	$11,717,502
$500	$40,835	$115,020	$249,790	$494,625	$939,420	$1,747,480	$3,215,475	$5,882,385	$10,727,346	$19,529,169

The Author

Dan Keppel has been helping people find financial services that fit their lifestyles since working in a securities firm, an insurer, two banks and his own "money coach" service. His book, *The Insiders' Guides to Buying Discount Financial Services:* Buy Direct and Save $3,000 Every Year, shows you how, what and where to buy financial products like industry insiders do—directly from the highest rated companies for less. He edits TheInsidersGuides.com and was an adjunct at a local college. He lives in Montclair, NJ with his wife, daughter and two cats, Anu and Katze.

Your ideas and suggestions are important. Share them at editor@TheInsiderSGuides.com.